Tools of the Trade

A Practical Guide for Trainers

By Linda Russell-Callecod

Copyright ©2007 Linda Russell-Callecod

Published by Seraphim Publications
PO Box 2023
Woodinville, WA 98072
info@seraphimpublications.net

Seraphim Publications

First Edition 2007

ISBN 978-1-933918-23-5

All rights reserved. This book may not be photocopied for personal or professional use. No part of this book may be reproduced, stored in a retrieval system, or transmitted in any form or by any means (electronic, mechanical, photocopying, recording, or otherwise) without permission in writing from the author or publisher.

*Dedicated to Ezra Casello, my long-time friend
and teaching inspiration, and my many trainers-in-training:
may each of you find fulfillment and joy as you make a difference
in the lives of others throughout your careers.*

*<u>Special thanks</u> to my husband Wayne
for his wonderful support and patience with me
during the creative process, and for suggesting the contents
of chapter one; to Dana Thompson, Sally Templeton, Linda Layton
and Dr. Kristina Hayek for sharing supportive feedback,
professional insights, and encouragement; to my
incredible sister and Muse, Janet Hayes for her
practical wisdom and most valuable input.*

"Example is not the main thing in influencing others.
It is the only thing."

Albert Schweitzer

Contents

Introduction vii

Tool #One: Personal Presence 1

Tool #Two: The Needs Assessment 7

Tool #Three: The Occupational Analysis 23

                  Scope and Sequence 26

Tool #Four: Objectives 29

                  Bloom's Taxonomy of Learning 33

Tool #Five: The Training Plan 39

Tool #Six: Instructional Methods and Materials 53

Tool #Seven: Master Mixes 63

Tool #Eight: Visual Aids 69

Tool #Nine: Evaluation 75

Tools in Action Review 81

Case Study: The Diversity Training Project 85

Case Study: The Making of a Training Academy 93

Appendix 109

- Tips for conducting focus group sessions
- Reproducible worksheets

References and Resources 119

v

About the Author

Linda Russell-Callecod is an executive consultant, keynote speaker, and master trainer/facilitator with a passion for training trainers, creating high performance teams, and developing leaders at all levels of the organization.

Linda began her professional life teaching and directing an adult music education program, and spent eleven years as a song writer and recording artist. Subsequent to that were three years as a junior high school teacher, and over twenty-five years working, teaching, and coaching in the field of retail - eleven of which were in human resources and people development.

Prior to becoming a partner with the Effectiveness Institute, a performance improvement consulting company in Redmond Washington, Linda was the Divisional Vice President of Training and Diversity for a major retailer where she founded an internal training academy, leaving a legacy which continues to develop and educate hundreds of employees in customer service, leadership, and technical skills.

Linda has designed curriculum for management and supervisory skills training, train-the-trainer programs, women's leadership development, and diversity awareness and efficacy.

She currently includes teaching for the University of Washington Extension Program as part of her long list of credits, and was honored as a recipient of their Teaching Excellence Award in Business and Management.

Linda realizes that when people go back to their jobs and continue exactly as they did prior to a training session it's a waste of everyone's time. She doesn't waste people's time. She blends a multiplicity of disciplines to create highly effective, interactive, supportive, and entertaining learning experiences, and has the talent to pass this skill on to others.

Linda currently lives with her husband, Wayne, in Woodinville Washington. Between them they have seven children and nine grandchildren.

Introduction

The role of training is more than teaching employees how to do their jobs, or assisting managers in managing more effectively. Its primary role is to help the organization solve business problems, and prepare for the future. Some of the challenges include: keeping pace with change, increasing business literacy within the organization, identifying and filling the leadership gap, finding cost-effective ways to develop people, correcting insufficient metrics, and effectively and efficiently utilizing new technology.

The corporate trainer is expected to help improve performance, which in turn increases productivity, customer satisfaction, profit, and (when done well) employee job satisfaction and retention. He/she is a leader, facilitator, teacher, consultant, administrator and coach – one who inspires and encourages others to take responsibility for their own learning and purposefully leads them through the process of discovery.

Trainers need to assess developmental requirements, then design, develop, and deliver the necessary training / instruction. In order to do this, the trainer must understand the business and its needs, and be able to articulate how those needs are linked to performance and learning. It is essential, therefore, that trainers develop business partnerships with managers at all levels of the organization – they are ultimately the key factor in the integration and overall success of the training. These partnerships do not happen because of the pleasant and "bubbly" personality of the trainer. The trainer must become a constant "student of the business," and become proficient at the skills and competencies that define the profession.[1]

In addition, the training professional must understand the various concepts and principles of adult learning. He / she must then create a process that results in a change of behavior in the participant that will ultimately lead to increased performance.

Although designed for the new trainer, this guide will provide the fundamental "tools of the trade" for skill and competency development of both the apprentice and the experienced.

---

[1] *The skills and competencies of the corporate trainer have been identified in Exhibit 3.2 Occupational Analysis Diagram, page 23.*

DIVERSITY MATTERS

It's important to understand that today's workplace is as diverse as the number of job functions within the organization. This has not only changed how companies chose to do business in order to stay competitive and attract the best talent, but also has changed how training is delivered. In addition to differences in behavior styles, learning styles, and competency levels, participants come with diversities of age, race, gender, ethnicity, language, abilities / disabilities, religious beliefs, and life styles.

The goal of the trainer is to create a learning environment in which participants feel safe, valued, and motivated to learn. In order to do this, it is *imperative* that as a training professional you are <u>first</u> honest with your own biases, and address them head-on. Your attitudes, beliefs, and preferences are subtly transferred to the classroom / workshop, and any insensitivity will have an adverse affect on your participants. If such a situation does happen and you are "called" on it, it is important to apologize immediately, express your empathy for any hurt or embarrassment, and ask for help in understanding.

Tool One: Personal Presence

One of the most important and powerful tools that a trainer has is <u>SELF</u>. Even with completing the most comprehensive needs assessment, identifying objectives with the greatest return-on-investment value, developing the most cutting-edge content, utilizing the best training methods possible, and having before you the most beautifully outlined training plan<u>, if no one finds you credible or likeable as the presenter, your mission will fail!</u>

Your personal presence – confidence, approachability, authenticity, and appearance – can "make or break" a session. Roger Ailes, the former media advisor to three US presidential campaigns says, "You are the message!" The message or content will fall on deaf ears if the messenger does not stir up conviction and confidence.

To obtain commitment to your program's initiatives and motivation to take action after a learning experience, participants must be <u>inspired</u>. To inspire is to "breathe" into them *spirit*, to infuse, to enliven, and to influence change. Your participants need to see and experience this in your leadership when you are before them.

The key is to maximize the "Who, the What, and the How" each time you stand before an audience to present.[1]

The Who is <u>You</u>: Give them the <u>appropriately authentic you</u> (be real and make it real for them)

The What is Your <u>Content</u>: Give them content they need and <u>makes them care</u>

The How is Your <u>Delivery</u>: Give them a format that <u>keeps them present</u>

Know your "Stuff" and <u>BE</u> the message.

Always be prepared and know your content - understand its theory, concepts and application as if it were your own. Also make it a habit to review the exercises and skill practices to the point that you can facilitate them naturally and easily. In other words, never create a situation where the participants have to wait for you to read and understand the material, or have to start and stop an exercise because the instructions were unclear or explained incorrectly.

As a trainer, you have a persona[2], and that persona should consist of an *expert professional* look with a *knowledgeable and approachable* style (look relatively formal; act reasonably informal)

1 *Excerpt from "Presentation Primer;" The Effectiveness Institute*
2. *Persona: the role one assumes or displays in public; one's public image or personality*

Your Look

John Molloy, in *Dress for Success* determined that business people who want to be successful have to achieve a certain professional "look." The first thing your participants will "scope out" is <u>you</u>. Within the first few seconds you enter the room, people will form an opinion that will often last the entire session. The way you dress provides their first clue as to what to expect, and their first indication and perception as to how the session will go. There *is* a professional "costume" that trainers must wear if they want to be taken seriously by others in the business world, yet there is still some individual character leeway within the costume parameters. One rule is to consider the audience, and dress "one step up."

> What people see is more powerful than what they hear.

For example, if you know that your participants will be dressed in business casual, then you can do likewise, but with an added jacket or sport coat.

With the increase of business casual attire or *casual Fridays* in the workplace, it is easy to let the conservative rules slide a bit. Nevertheless, you have a specific role to fill as the training leader, and you must also dress the part. Any carelessness in dress or hygiene - including the clean but sloppy look – can cause participants to wonder if your session will also be careless, sloppy, and/or offensive. You want to portray an image that says you can be trusted to lead the group through the learning process, and that you want your participants to take it as seriously as you.

Here are some simple guidelines:

- Dress appropriately professional and comfortable, including hair and makeup – look like you're worth it

- Make sure your clothing fits well and that you can move in easily (not too tight or revealing)

- Avoid wearing anything distracting, such as heavy gaudy accessories

- Don't let your clothes "upstage" your presentation (the group should remember what you taught them, not what you wore)

- Avoid overpowering your participants with colors that are *too* bright and fragrances that are too strong

- Wear comfortable shoes (I realize that often female participants will notice your shoes and make judgments accordingly. In order to balance the practical-comfortable with the stylish-expected, I will often wear one pair of shoes to meet, greet, and provide introductions, then at the break I wear what I know can actually stand in for 8 hours – just an option.)

Your Style

This is all about being able to *connect* with your audience. My sister Janet, who is also a consultant and trainer (yes it runs in the family), greets the participants at the door, introduces herself, and allows them to get comfortable with her <u>before</u> the session begins, rather than *during* the session. As simple as it may seem, this is a powerful technique.

Realize it or not, a trainer gets "reviewed" by all the participants in a session, and sometimes to the point of it determining for them whether to believe the content or not. A perfect 5.0 rating on your evaluation is wonderful to have, but generally speaking a 4.3 – 4.5 is a good indication that your style was working. One person's opinion may not be helpful information, but if an entire classroom of participants gives a similar review, you know where you stand. Although your style must <u>always</u> be authentic, (the real you) it is important to modify your style to fit your content and audience.

One advantage of perfecting your training persona is that it enables you to be objective. This objectivity is particularly important for trainers because it allows them to adapt and modify their training style without betraying "self," and keeps hurt feelings and depression at a minimum when/if someone criticizes them. Negative comments can be taken professionally and not personally, and the trainer can re-examine their persona to determine what adjustments must be made.

For instance, an entertaining, energetic, and enthusiastic persona can help keep lower to mid-level employees alert and engaged through several hours of training. When giving the same content to senior-level managers with a shorter time frame, this high-charged style could very well be a turn-off. Take your cue from your audience.

Your persona is the first visual the audiences sees, and remember: what people see is more powerful than what they hear. Again, it can affect how they react to you personally and how they react to the learning experience.

> "I give the same mashed potatoes for each speech. I just change the gravy."
>
> Dr. Norman Vincent Peale

GESTURES, FACIAL EXPRESSIONS, AND BODY LANGUAGE

Your gestures, facial expressions, and body language all impact your participants' perception of you. They can either encourage listening and involvement, or discourage participants from engaging in the session.

"The secret to successful public speaking is just what your mother always told you: 'Stand up straight, look people in the eye, and stop fidgeting.'" [3]

[3] *Anonymous; from "The Standup Trainer" (1995)*

As I mentioned before in my sister's example, it is very important that trainers establish an immediate rapport with their participants – I can't emphasize this enough. Your two best techniques for this are eye contact and conversation. This is why trainers often begin their sessions by asking participants their name, job title, and expectations for the class. When used as an opening, it sets an informal and conversational tone for the session, and sends a message to the participants that the trainer's goal is to make the experience fit their needs. Janet explains, "Once I've established a relationship with the participants, discussions for them are like fire-side chats, and not like oral exams."

Gestures

Gestures should flow naturally and add meaningful emphasis to your words, not detract from the presentation. In Hamlet's admonishment to the *Players*, he said "Suit the action to the word; the word to the action." Gestures must not send a message of their own.

Trainers who stand frozen to one spot and use very little (or strained) gestures send a message that "It's ok to close your eyes and nap, for there will be nothing interesting to look at here."

The other extreme is the trainer who flails his/her arms wildly and exaggerates movements. This person sends an equally disturbing message: "You won't be able to look here for very long without becoming exhausted and having your eyes go crossed." Your goal is to find an *authentic* middle-ground.

Facial Expressions

One of a trainer's greatest assets is his/her smile. The first time your participants see you, they must see and feel your warmth, approachability, and sincerity. Smile with both your mouth and your eyes (having direct eye contact at the time helps significantly). Like with gestures, throughout your session your facial expressions can help or hinder your effectiveness. Make sure they remain harmonious with your message, but most of all make sure you *have* expression.

Body Language

How you stand and move signals your level of confidence (or over confidence). Here's a tip: stand straight with your feet shoulder-length apart to give you balance and avoid swaying. Maintaining eye contact with your audience provides an opportunity for you to stay "in tune" with their feelings and responses, and is a compelling means for establishing rapport. Then, let your movements flow naturally and logically throughout the session.

Review Quiz

1. What is the most powerful tool the trainer has available?
   _____

2. What three things must a presenter remember to maximize each time he/she presents?

   1)

   2)

   3)

3. What are the two primary characteristics of an effective trainer's persona?

   1)

   2)

4. What is an advantage to perfecting your training persona?
   _____

5. There really is no specific dress code for trainers, but the "rule of thumb" would be to dress the same way your participants dress in order to fit in. True or False? _____

6. It is important for you to always be authentic and present the unmodified "real you," even if your style does not work well with your audience. Your participants will eventually adjust to you. True or False? _____

7. What are the best two techniques for establishing rapport with your participants?

   1)

   2)

8. What is a trainer's most valuable asset? _____

---

1. His/herself; 2. The who, what, how or you, content, delivery; 3. an expert professional look, a knowledgeable yet approachable style; 4. You can be objective or objectivity; 5; false; 6. False; 7. Eye contact and conversation; 8. His/ her smile.

Personal Notes

Tool Two: The Needs Assessment

The purpose of a needs assessment is to prevent "putting a band-aid on an ulcer," or applying a quick-fix to an organizational performance *symptom* rather than curing the illness (solving the problem). If the right questions are answered, the needs assessment will make certain that your solution addresses the real issues, and focuses your time, resources, and efforts on objective versus subjective results.

With very few exceptions, the books on training will tell you NEVER to create a training program or curriculum without a needs assessment. Some will even say not to begin training at *all* without an assessment. Determining your training needs *is* the first step in creating a successful training program, but conducting a full-blown assessment may NOT be your answer.

For example, if your organization has integrated a new IT system[1] that affects the way a large number of employees do their job, you don't need a formal assessment to tell you that there's a training need. Logically, you know that employees will need to be trained on the new system in order to understand and effectively use the technology.

Conversely, doing training for the sake of training when there is no justifiable necessity wastes time, energy, and most of all dollars. It may also hurt your credibility as a training professional.

IDENTIFYING WHEN AN ASSESSMENT IS NEEDED

There are a number of indicators that signal possible training needs:

- ***Poor performance.*** Although an indicator of possible training needs, poor performance may be symptomatic of poor management practices, inadequate systems, outdated equipment, or organizational barriers. A needs assessment will help determine whether the problem requires a training or non-training solution.

- ***Change.*** Training is a solution to specific performance problems and most problems are caused by something changing. When an organization experiences change (whether internal or external), *especially* if it includes changes to its business operations, there is a good chance that some type of training will be needed.

[1] *Information Technology: the development, installation, and implementation of computer systems and applications.*

Types of Change

- *Internal changes:*
  - New products or services
  - New equipment / technology
  - Changes in standards
  - New policies or procedures
  - Promotions and employee job changes

- *External changes:*
  - Changing economy
  - Government regulations
  - Changing demographics and employee expectations

- **Insufficient metrics[2] / measurements.** When there are no adequate standard of performance measurements in place, such as dashboards[3] or performance scorecards[4], a needs assessment can provide a *baseline* against which to measure results or changes going forward.

It provides the foundation for program development and <u>sets the criteria for measuring the success of the program</u> at its completion. In layman's terms it means that the needs assessment will identify the conditions of "where you are," to allow to you to measure these conditions against where you really *want* to be.

A training needs assessment looks for organizational training needs without assuming that training is the "answer" until the need has been clearly identified.

THE NEEDS-ASSESSMENT PROCESS

The assessment process will help you identify the level of performance, or the situation as it exists in the "now" (current state), and where you want to be instead (desired state). Once completed, it will also help identify the barriers, and the gap between the current and desired states - which becomes your potential training need, and the basis for your training design.

1. *A standard to measure critical success factors.*
2. *A system to track and monitor key performance indicators (values on a measurement scale or continuum – how much and to what extent)*
3. *Statistics derived by summarizing raw data into important performance trends*

The needs assessment process should never be a "loner" activity. You must involve other people in the process in order to ensure that you get the information you need. People like to be asked what they think. If they believe you will take their input seriously, they will offer far more useful information. Involvement inspires commitment, and those who help you in the process become partners in shaping the solution. These are the individuals who can be your strongest supporters as you move towards implementation and results.

The Needs-Assessment Process has seven action steps:

1. Identify the Problem
2. Determine the Assessment Audience (who needs to be asked what?)
3. Determine the Method(s) of Analysis
4. Collect Data
5. Sort and Analyze Data
6. Communicate Feedback and Results
7. Determine Next Steps

1. Identify the Problem. Because the purpose of training is to help solve organizational problems, you must have a clear understanding of what the business problems are. If possible, find out what the problem is costing the organization in lost business, errors, turnover, etc. Remember, the potential training need is represented in the gap existing between the desired state and the current state.

Example

Current State: The ABC Widget Company is producing 50 fair-quality widgets an hour. Because of this, they are unable to meet high customer demands and are increasingly losing market share. The XYZ Widget and Digit Company across town is producing 125 high-quality widgets an hour for $1.00 less per unit.

Desired State: The ABC Widget Company wants to be the preferred supplier of widgets. It wants to regain the market share lost to the XYZ Company and increase it by 10%.

The Gap: ABC Company is producing 75 widgets per hour less than its competitor; its fair-quality standard is far below the potential "highest" quality desired; the costs associated with production and/or distribution are $1.00 higher per unit than the competition. <u>This is a problem that is costing the company $250,000 per quarter in revenue and a 50% drop in the employee satisfaction survey.</u>

In this example, the potential training needs that may solve the ABC Company's problem may be one or more of the following:

- Skill development to increase employees' ability to make high quality widgets

- Training to increase proficiency and therefore reduce errors that create re-dos or waste

- Skill training for supervisors who manage poorly

- Teambuilding to increase synergy on the team and increase employee motivation

- None of the above

Until you analyze what *caused* the gap, or the *reason* for the gap, you still may miss the mark.

2. Determine the Assessment Audience: Who to Assess. The level and depth of your assessment determines who you'll select to survey. Consider the groups listed below in deciding who may be best in providing the necessary and appropriate data.

Senior Executives. This group can provide the "big picture" perspective of the problems, and their impact on the business. They can also supply information on any potential industry changes and identify the direction the organization is taking.

Human Resources. Your HR department is your best resource for records and documents. They can supply you with data from performance appraisals, exit interviews, grievances, turnover, safety violations, and so forth.

The Targeted Training Audience. It is of the utmost importance to involve the targeted audience. They will be able to provide information on both their perceived and real training needs. If they are over looked, they will not have a sense of "buy-in" and may be resistant and resentful.

Managers of the Targeted Audience. Since one of the objectives of training is helping managers to solve business problems, the manager can supply important information in assessment of training needs.

Direct Reports. When the targeted audience is supervisors and managers, their direct reports can provide valuable insight into the skills and competencies that need improvement.

Vendors. Vendors are an external resource that can provide an objective perspective. In addition, they may be able to supply information on industry standards and norms.

Customers. Survey data from internal and external customers can provide quantitative information that can help identify deficiencies in the quality of service and products.

Industry Experts. These experts can identify the industry best practices and standards by which you can compare and measure your organization's effectiveness and competitiveness.

3. Determine the Method(s) of Analysis. Now that the problem has been identified, the next step is to determine the _cause(s)_ of the problem or gap - not just the symptoms. For this, it is best to use several tools and techniques. Choose your method based on the appropriateness to the problem, time, costs, trust level, validity, complexity, workplace disruption, and available resources.

Develop a systematic approach as to how you will gather and record the data. Make sure the process is standardized and organized. This will make it easier for you to retrieve the information when you are ready to analyze the results.

1) First, establish and verify the appropriate assessment method(s) available

2) Secondly, determine the advantages / disadvantages of the method(s)

Types of Methods

There are many assessment methods available to provide you with data that will help you determine the training needs of your organization. Some of the considerations you must take into account before selecting your methodology include: the level of trust with respondents (are they "gun-shy" of surveys because of previous negative experiences?), the cost of analysis and execution, the number of people involved, and to what extent information is already accessible.

Assessment methods generally fall into six types:

1. Open-ended surveys
2. Closed-ended surveys
3. Interviews
4. Review of existing records / data
5. Survey instruments (see Ex 2.2 and 2.3)
6. Observation

What's best for another organization may not be best for you. However there are some up-sides and down-sides to each (see table 2.1)

2.1

	Up-Side	**Down-Side**
Open-ended Surveys	Inexpensive; individuals will provide more detailed information; effective with focus groups when used verbally; easy to create	Takes longer to analyze data; individuals may be reluctant to put comments in writing; less objective, more vague
Closed-ended Questionnaires	Faster and easier to complete; inexpensive; can be anonymous	Gain limited information; possible misinterpretation of questions; takes more time to design well
Interviews, including focus groups	Able to read non-verbal communication; builds relationships; gains more details – able to probe; easier to talk	Takes more time to conduct; possible bias of interviewer; more difficult to analyze; loss of anonymity
Reviewing Existing Records / Data	Information already exists; easy to access; inexpensive; discreet and unpretentious	Information may be out of date; perhaps too generic; risk of bias; may not include exact data needed; cannot probe for more information
Surveys, including tests and skill assessments	Validated by research; easy to score; moderately easy to conduct	Needs administration; difficult to self-construct; may be expensive
Observation	Real-life data; low cost	Time consuming; difficult to organize and analyze data

Less common assessment methods may include:

- Industry bench-marking
- Inventorying existing training offerings and evaluating their effectiveness
- 360º Assessment
- Job /Occupational Analysis (described in chapter 3)

Questions an Effective Assessment Should Answer

You know that you have appropriately designed your assessment methodology if it answers the following questions:

- What is the cause of the performance / behavioral gap?
- What is needed to "Close the Gap?"
- Is training needed?
- *Who* needs training and why?
- What type of training / development is needed?
- How much, or to what extent is training needed?
- What is the level of receptivity in the organization?

As a training professional, it is important that you become familiar and comfortable with a wide variety of assessment tools. This will allow you to select the "right tool for the right job."

Ex 2.2 *Sample* **Training Survey: Management / Supervisory Skills**

Instructions: Please help us identify key training needs by providing your honest opinions. Circle the rating which best describes the importance of the skill to your job, and your level of satisfaction in your ability to perform that skill. Your answers will remain anonymous.

Rating Scale Values: 0 = Not at all; **1** = Very Little; **2** = Somewhat; **3** = Very Much; **4** = Extremely; N/A = Not Applicable

	Question	Rating Scale						
1.	Communicating with direct reports / staff	Importance	0	1	2	3	4	N/A
		Satisfaction	0	1	2	3	4	N/A
2.	Creating a work environment where team members of varying backgrounds and work styles feel accepted and valued	Importance	0	1	2	3	4	N/A
		Satisfaction	0	1	2	3	4	N/A
3.	Resolving difficult issues and important problems	Importance	0	1	2	3	4	N/A
		Satisfaction	0	1	2	3	4	N/A
4.	Motivating direct reports / staff	Importance	0	1	2	3	4	N/A
		Satisfaction	0	1	2	3	4	N/A
5.	Career planning for direct reports / staff	Importance	0	1	2	3	4	N/A
		Satisfaction	0	1	2	3	4	N/A
6.	Creating and managing teams	Importance	0	1	2	3	4	N/A
		Satisfaction	0	1	2	3	4	N/A
7.	Presentation skills	Importance	0	1	2	3	4	N/A
		Satisfaction	0	1	2	3	4	N/A
8.	Managing change	Importance	0	1	2	3	4	N/A
		Satisfaction	0	1	2	3	4	N/A
9.	Assessing and appraising direct reports / staff	Importance	0	1	2	3	4	N/A
		Satisfaction	0	1	2	3	4	N/A
10.	Financial management	Importance	0	1	2	3	4	N/A
		Satisfaction	0	1	2	3	4	N/A
11.	Interviewing techniques and skill	Importance	0	1	2	3	4	N/A
		Satisfaction						
12.	Project management	Importance	0	1	2	3	4	N/A
		Satisfaction	0	1	2	3	4	N/A

Ex2.3 *Sample* Training Survey: Sales

Instructions: Please help us identify key training needs by providing your honest opinions. Circle the rating which best describes the importance of the skill to your job, and your level of satisfaction in your ability to perform that skill. Your answers will remain anonymous.

Rating Scale Values: **0**= Not at all; **1**= Very Little; **2**= Somewhat; **3** = Very Much; **4** = Extremely; N/A = Not Applicable

	Question	Rating Scale						
1.	Good questioning skills	Importance	0	1	2	3	4	N/A
		Satisfaction	0	1	2	3	4	N/A
2.	Negotiation skills	Importance	0	1	2	3	4	N/A
		Satisfaction	0	1	2	3	4	N/A
3.	Handling objections	Importance	0	1	2	3	4	N/A
		Satisfaction	0	1	2	3	4	N/A
4.	Controlling conversations	Importance	0	1	2	3	4	N/A
		Satisfaction	0	1	2	3	4	N/A
5.	Cold calling techniques	Importance	0	1	2	3	4	N/A
		Satisfaction	0	1	2	3	4	N/A
6.	Reading non-verbal communication	Importance	0	1	2	3	4	N/A
		Satisfaction	0	1	2	3	4	N/A
7.	Influencing skills	Importance	0	1	2	3	4	N/A
		Satisfaction	0	1	2	3	4	N/A
8.	Presentation skills	Importance	0	1	2	3	4	N/A
		Satisfaction	0	1	2	3	4	N/A
9.	Communicating with vendors / suppliers	Importance	0	1	2	3	4	N/A
		Satisfaction	0	1	2	3	4	N/A
10.	Financial management	Importance	0	1	2	3	4	N/A
		Satisfaction	0	1	2	3	4	N/A
11.	Report writing	Importance	0	1	2	3	4	N/A
		Satisfaction	0	1	2	3	4	N/A

What specific training needs do you have that are not covered on this form?

Selecting or Purchasing a Published Assessment Instrument

There are many excellent published assessment instruments and tools available. The problem is often selecting the appropriate instrument to meet your and your organization's need. Following are some informational guidelines that will assist in your decision making. (See the Appendix for a list of assessment resources.)

There are six assessment instrument types that fall into two categories:

The Perception Category (five types)

1. What the organization is, as perceived by those completing the instrument

2. What the job is, as perceived by those completing the instrument

3. What/who an individual is, as a self-perception and by others' evaluation

4. What an individual does, as perceived by self and others

5. What an individual values, as perceived by self and others

The Knowledge-based Category (one type)

6. What an individual knows, as demonstrated by their knowledge in completing the instrument

In conducting a training needs assessment, the **Perception Instrument** is generally a multiple-choice questionnaire used to determine which of a list of topics are perceived as being training needs; e.g.: "Which of the following communication skills listed do you feel are most needed in your company's training program?"

There are several advantages to using this type of instrument. Generally speaking, they are simple to administer, quick and easy to complete, easy to score, and can be taken by all levels of the organization.

The disadvantage is that perception instruments are easy to manipulate. If, for example, I think my job stability or promotability may be affected by my responses (my needs), I may check those things that would make me look the best in the company's eyes. In addition, what people perceive they know, do, and need is often different from what they *really* know, do, and need

The **Knowledge-based Instrument** is used to identify a targeted population's knowledge in specific areas of competency. They may also be easy to administer, but dissimilar from the perception instrument in that it is harder to manipulate. As a result, this instrument usually provides more accurate data.

Some of the down-sides of the knowledge-based instrument are that employees often experience "testing anxieties," they are harder to score (sometimes necessary to be scored by the supplier or via expensive electronic equipment / software), and take longer to complete.

Rule(s) of thumb:

1. Don't create your own test if you can buy one (they are much harder to create than one might think), and when you're looking to purchase one, look for the number of specific topics covered by the instrument.

2. Make sure you compare the information the instrument is ascertaining to the information you need to know in order to address your organization's needs. (Consider the questions on page 8: "Questions an Effective Assessment Should Answer.")

3. For multiple-topic assessments, make sure that each topic is sub-scored.

4. Check the published figures for reliability and validity, making sure that they are published norms (results from other organizations when they were assessed), giving you the opportunity to compare your score with theirs, and providing more information about your group.

5. The courts are concerned with *content* validity (whether the questions match the subject matter they are supposed to measure). To this end, make sure that the instrument you select has links between the tasks of the job, the task-related behaviors, and the questions it asks.

6. Consider the costs. There are excellent multiple-topic instruments that you can purchase in the $30 - $60 range, while there are also others that can run as high as several hundred dollars per person. Do your homework ahead of time.

4. Collect Data. The method you use to collect data is directly linked to the assessment format or method you have chosen. This can range from electronic reports complied and written after focus group interviews, or data generated by an outsourced organization and provided to you in charts, graphs, and summary reports. Sometimes it is not only important to examine the needs of the organization internally, but to consider outside reports as well. Most often, using a *variety* of methods is best.

Whichever methods are used, you have a responsibility to communicate to your respondents[4] how the information will be used and what information will or will not remain confidential.

Continue to expand your partnerships by including others as information gatherers as well as respondents.

5. Sort and Analyze Data. Sorting your information is the core of your needs assessment. By condensing your data into a manageable, categorical form before interpreting it, you will be able to simplify what could be a very complex procedure. The prioritization process is important because your assessment will probably result in a long list of training needs, some of which you may not be able to provide.

For qualitative data (interviews, focus groups, observations, questionnaires, etc.), do a content analysis and identify common themes. The objective is to categorize and quantify the information as much as possible with minimal interpretation.

For quantitative data (assessment instruments, closed-ended questionnaires, etc.), do a statistical analysis[5] Be careful not to become over-analytical with the number-crunching process - keep it simple. Look at the data in terms of averages, medians (the middle number within a group), and modes (the number that occurs most often).

If your analysis dictates that training is needed, be specific as to the type of training required. Training must address the problem specifically, and the organizational systems must be in place to support the outcomes. If your analysis concluded that the issues that need addressing are *not* training issues at all, you must still share that information with your best recommendations.

---

[4] *Your respondents include all the individuals who participated in your assessment surveys, interviews, and questionnaires. This does not include those whose archived documents were reviewed.*

[5] *A numerical format that tells you how many, how much, and to what extent*

Interpreting the information is not always an easy process. You must use both your intellect and perceptions to develop useful recommendations.

Review:

- Conduct qualitative analysis

- Conduct quantitative analysis

- Establish partnerships (HR, Subject-matter-experts, etc.) in determining solutions and recommendations

6. Communicate Feedback and Results. After you have completed the data analysis and have identified the training needs, design a strategy (action plan) and prepare to share your process, conclusions, and recommendations with key shareholders[6]. In their book, *Figuring Things Out*, Zemke and Kramlinger state "The quality of a result's presentation is more important than the quality of the study that produced the results." They are right.

Even the best assessment results and subsequent recommendations when presented poorly, have barely a hope and a prayer of being approved and adopted. Therefore, it is extremely important that you plan and craft your presentation with care.

Remember, your objective is to present the information in a way that will move you forward toward approval and/or support for your proposal. The "numbers" or the data will NOT speak for itself, no matter how sophisticated the assessment tool. Your job is to present the data in the most meaningful and insightful way possible.

There are two things to consider when preparing your feedback: what to share and how to share it.

---

[6] *Your shareholders include anyone in the organization who serves to gain from the successful outcomes of the training, or suffer loss if it does not occur, and/or the individual(s) who requested your training help. This includes the person(s) funding the training with dollars and/or resources.*

a. *What to share.* There are six steps in sharing your feedback:

1. Describe the method(s) and process you used in conducting your needs analysis

2. Present the raw data

3. Identify the key issues by objectively presenting your analysis

4. Describe potential and probable employee expectations

5. Identify barriers

6. Present your recommendations

b. *How to share.* Your final report is critical and should be delivered in both an oral and written format. It must be positive and encouraging, always offering confidence in your plan to address organizational needs and measurable results.

- The **written report** must be constructed in an easy-to-understand format. The length will depend on the extent of the assessment.

    - Provide a concise one-page executive overview to key decision makers. Include:
        o The description of the process
        o A summary of your findings
        o An objective analysis of the data, your recommendations (make a strong link to the business need)
        o Identification of any potential barriers.

- The **oral presentation** is an opportunity to sell your ideas and to enhance your credibility.

When planning your presentation, clearly identify your objectives: giving information, obtaining reactions, soliciting ideas, gaining management buy-in and approval for your recommendations, and securing the commitment for *future* recommendations.

- Be objective when presenting the data; be concise yet accurate

- Manage your time: do not "over-talk" or use jargon

- Use strong visuals or charts to support your data and to meet the style needs of your audience

- Be prepared for questions and challenges, and have the raw data on hand as back up

7. Determine Next Steps. The last step in the needs assessment process is to translate your recommendations into a plan of action – the training approach. This is not the training design, but rather a description of the training needed that will resolve the issues. Include specific action items with a time line and task assignments. You may include training objectives, methods, and available trainers.

Review Quiz

1. There are three primary indicators that signal possible training needs. Name one: _____

2. Identify the seven steps of the needs assessment process.

    1)

    2)

    3)

    4)

    5)

    6)

    7)

3. An effective needs assessment should answer several important questions, one of which is whether training is needed. True or False? _____

4. Name three assessment methods.

    1)

    2)

    3)

5. What is the difference between a Perception-jbased and a Knowledge-based Assessment Instrument?

    _____

    _____

6. Regardless of how you present your analysis and recommendations to key stakeholders, having your data detailed and well organized is what will matter most. True or False? _____

---

1. Poor performance; change; or insufficient metrics. 2. Identify the problem; Determine assessment audience; Determine the methods; Collect data; Sort & analyze data; Communicate results; Determine next steps. 3. True 4. Any of the following: interviews, questionnaires, tests, focus groups, observations, survey instruments, occupational analysis, bench-marking, 360^0 reviews, reports. 5. Perception instruments identify the perceptions of the audience, Knowledge-based instruments assesses what respondents know. 6. False

Tool Three: The Occupational Analysis with Scope and Sequence

An occupational analysis is a type of needs assessment that determines, more specifically, the potential training needs of a group of employees with a common job function (a multi-incumbent group). It is used when needing to create a developmental curriculum for the first time (even when there may or may *not* be an organizational problem), or when needing to develop improved performance support systems and training strategies for a specific group.

The occupational analysis is a process of dissecting the responsibilities and tasks of a specific job / occupation and extrapolating the skills and competencies necessary to perform that job – from the simple to the complex. This process may also prove valuable for determining performance standards and expectations for the multi-incumbent group.

The Process:

1) Identify the job and the prerequisites – the minimally required skill-sets brought to the job

2) Provide a brief overview of primary function(s) – the Dictionary of Occupational Titles ("DOT") may be helpful: www.occupationalinfo.org

3) List the specific tasks performed as part of the normal activities of this job

4) Identify the competencies[1] needed to fulfill the tasks from simple to mastery level

A comprehensive occupational analysis will result in a hierarchy of tasks with associated skills and competencies including:

- Cognitive skills[2] (the knowledge level or "thinking" ability necessary to successfully complete the task)

- Affective competencies (value-based behaviors and beliefs that impact a person's attitude)

- Psychomotor / Kinesthetic skills (the physical abilities necessary to complete the task)

These elements can be arranged on a chart to graphically depict the relationship between job components, job intellect, and capability. This chart is called the *Occupational Analysis Diagram* (exhibits 3.1 and 3.2).

---

[1]*Competencies: having suitable or sufficient skill, knowledge, experience, etc.*

[2]*For a greater understanding of learning competencies and levels, see Bloom's Taxonomy of Learning, chapter 4*

Once the skills have been identified, they are prioritized by skill mastery level and integrated into a developmental strategy. (See Exhibit 3.3: *Scope and Sequence*)

Data Gathering

In order to avoid making assumptions about the job and its functions, the training professional should not rely solely on subject-matter-experts for information. Interviewing supervisors, career consultants, and internal customers can provide a more comprehensive understanding of what that job does and how it is done.

Ex 3.1
Occupational Analysis Diagram

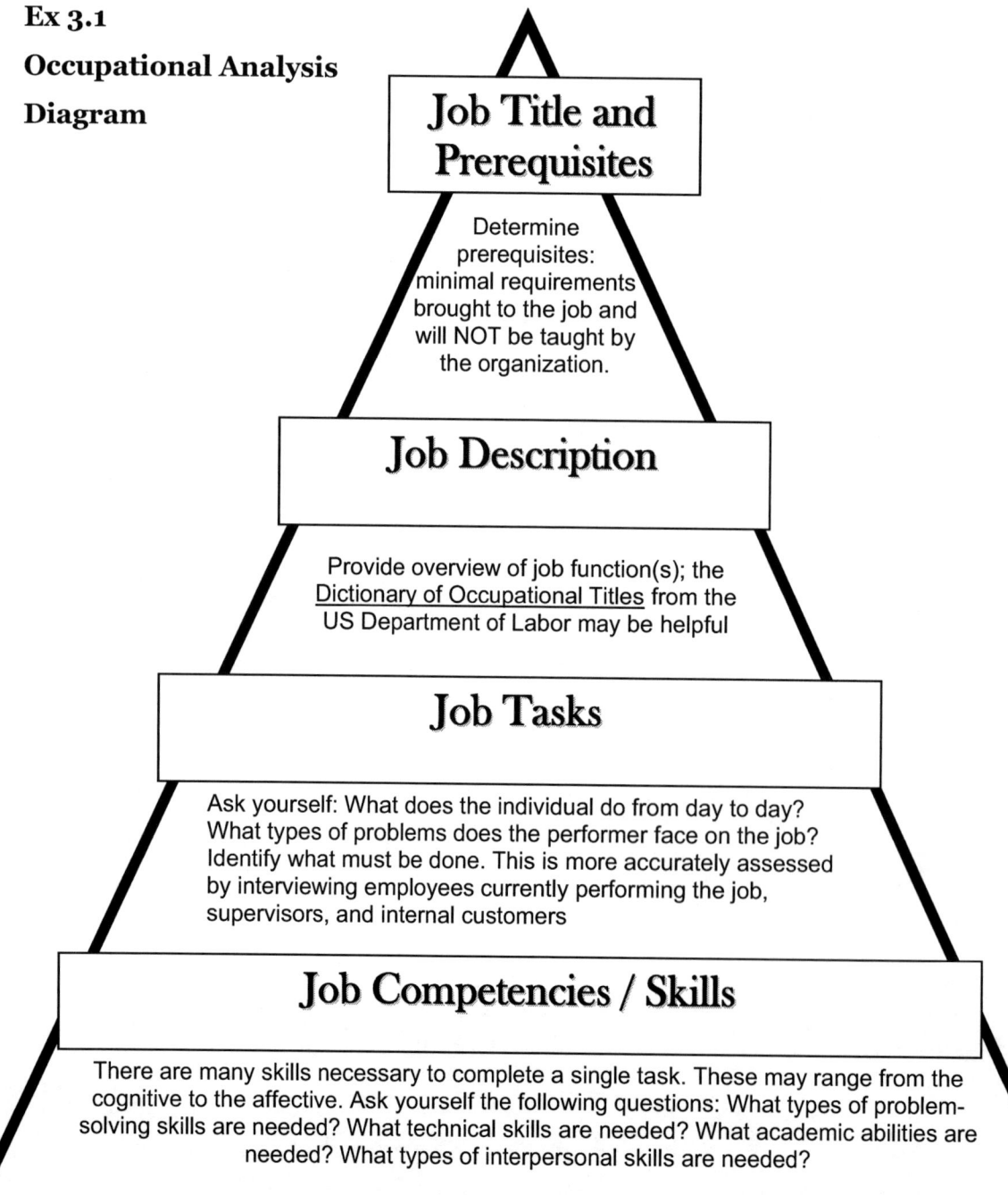

Ex 3.2   **Occupational Analysis Diagram**

Corporate Training Manager

Prerequisite: Requires a college degree and 3-5 years training experience.

Job Description: Oversees training (and development) within an organization. Ensures that employees are developed to their highest potential. Sets learning goals within the organization. Supervises training staff. Provides planning and/or input into budget and cost controls.

Tasks

Develops curriculum and courses based on job needs/functions; teaches/facilitates classroom instruction; conducts classroom audits for course/classroom effectiveness; facilitates meetings and focus groups; plans and participates in annual recognition programs; builds external business partnerships; troubleshoots; consults; provides in-service training for other trainers and staff; prepares budget and determines allocation of funds for staff, supplies, and equipment and facilities; prepares, creates and analyzes data from questionnaires, interviews and group discussions to evaluate curriculums, teaching methods, and community participation; recruits and develops classroom trainers and/or subject matter experts; schedules classes and classroom logistics; tracks, assesses and rewards participant and staff trainer development; reports program results to stakeholders and/or executive board; participates in corporate training-team meetings and activities; executes training priorities from "corporate"; determines external "vendor" involvement and hires/purchases external programs.

Competencies/Skills

Know and apply instructional system design and development principles (able to write clear and appropriate course curriculum); able to "multi task"; able to effectively lead people and manage several projects at once; negotiation/influencing skills; project management skills; accounting/expense management skills; analytical skills; time management skills; speaks (English) well/articulate; demonstrate relaxed and confident platform and presentation skills; communicate effectively in writing; able to lead a team/build trust and confidence; able to construct and deliver a business report; strategic thinking and consulting skills; able to assess organizational/departmental program needs; evaluate the instructional design, development and delivery function(s); assure the application of effective training principles; assure preparation of the instructional site; establish and maintain instructor credibility; use media and "visuals" effectively; evaluate learner performance; manage the learning environment; respond appropriately to learner's needs; link human performance to the effectiveness of the organization; think critically when making decisions and solving problems; produce effective and efficient "solutions"; develop and sustain social relationships; adapt strategies and solutions in a "rapid change" environment and industry.

Ex 3.3 Sample Scope and Sequence of Skill Mastery: Corporate Training Manager

Mastery				
	Effective negotiations; Adapt strategies & solutions in a rapidly changing environment.	Ability to determine "outsourcing strategies	Conduct expense analysis and plan annual budgets	Link human resource performance to the effectiveness of the organization
	Apply instructional system design & development principles	Ability to influence at all levels; Skills to hire and develop staff	Evaluate instructional design, development, and delivery functions; Ability to lead and instruct peers	Strategic thinking and consulting skills; Internal "political" savvy
	Teach / instruct instructors; Recruit & recognize volunteers	Skilled project management ability; Able to create business reports; Able to assess organizational / dept. program needs (including creating needs assessment tools)	Ability to develop and sustain positive business & social relationships – high level of Emotional Intelligence; Able to assess SME ability / aptitude; Able to manage and resolve conflict	Able to think critically when making decisions and problem solving; effective team leadership
Inter-mediate	Word processing and PowerPoint expertise; Able to communicate effectively in writing; Establish and maintain instructor credibility; Able to prioritize	Able to multi-task; High level of organizational skills; Able to assure the application of effective training principles; Assure preparation of instructional site and logistics	Basic analytical & math skills: effective use of "Excel;" Ability to stay focused	Ability to write clear and appropriate course curriculum; Ability to work under pressure
Basic / Entry	Speaks (English) well – articulate; Ability to write clearly on flipcharts; Ability to use and create training visuals effectively; Ability to read aloud with expression and ease; Ability to learn	Good time management skills; Able to use multi-media resources appropriately and effectively; Good people skills; Able to give and take directions	Able to demonstrate relaxed and confident platform and presentation skills; Able to evaluate learner's performance	Able to manage a diverse learning environment; Able to respond appropriately to learner's needs

Low → High

SKILL CONTINUUM

Review Quiz

1. What reason would one have for conducting an occupational analysis?

   _____

   _____

   _____

2. Identify the four steps to creating an occupational analysis.

   a.

   b.

   c.

   d.

3. The best resource for identifying the tasks related to the job you want to analyze is the subject-matter-expert. True or False? _____

Matching

_____ 1. Affective Competency   a) The physical abilities necessary to complete a task.

_____ 2. Cognitive Skills   b) Value based behaviors and beliefs that impact attitude.

_____ 3. Psychomotor /Kinesthetic Skills   c) The knowledge level or "thinking" ability necessary to successfully complete the task.

---

1. When there is a new position created for a multi-incumbent group, or developing improved performance systems; 2. a) Identify the job and prerequisites b) Provide overview of job functions c) Identify tasks d) Identify skills / competencies; 3. False; 4. b, c, a

> Learners want to know that the training program is relevant to their needs. Remember to assess your potential audience to capture their perception of their needs, desires and expectations.
>
> Participants will not learn just because you are presenting the material. Adult learners are motivated by their own reasons and definitions of value – not yours.

ASTD Info-line *Do's and Don'ts for the New Trainer (1996)*

Tool Four: Objectives

A training objective is simply the detailed description of the intended outcomes for the learning experience – your target. It will describe the observable behaviors, the conditions in which the learner can/will perform, the level of productivity, and in the case of a program objective, the value added to the organization. It is also the first step in creating a training plan, and will answer the question: "What will participants be able to do, think, or feel differently as a result of the training?"

Your program objectives function as a blueprint for your training design, and for your participants, the learning objectives serve as a contract between them and the instructor. By having clear objectives, the instructor/ trainer is able to stay focused on the outcomes of the learning experience and utilize the appropriate methods to accomplish the goal. In turn, the participants will know what's in it for them (WIIFM[1]), know what to expect from the instructor, and what is expected of them in the learning process.

Note: Training objectives must describe the "end" rather than the "means" – a final product not a process. They are also written from the participant's perspective and not the instructors; e.g. "Participants will be able to..." instead of "I will demonstrate to the participants how to..."

> "Students need to know that they are responsible for learning."
>
> Martin M. Broadwell

Writing the *Right* Objective for the *Right* Plan

There's a difference between writing an objective for a training curriculum or program that includes seven (7) different courses, than writing a learning objective for a single course, or for the individual modules within a course. The difference lies in the scope[2,] and the audience for which it is intended.

The Program Objective addresses the issues/problems uncovered in the needs assessment. It describes what will be different after *all* courses have been completed: what will be different for the participant, different for the organization, and different in terms of solving the "problem." The Program Objective is written primarily for the instructor and the company /or training stakeholders[3].

---

[1] "What's in it for me?"

[2] Relates to the extent, amount of area covered, the range, and breadth of the training program's impact

[3] The ones who are paying for/supporting the training effort or requested the training help

> **Ex 4.1 Program Objective**
>
> At the end of this program, mid-managers will be able to <u>manage</u> the production of a high quality widget with a productivity rate of 125 units per hour; <u>demonstrate</u> sensitivity towards individual and cultural differences; <u>integrate</u> their acquired knowledge of behavior and communication styles, team development, and conflict resolution to <u>create</u> high performing teams; <u>analyze</u> and <u>solve</u> problems more effectively thereby reducing the escalation of issues; and <u>demonstrate</u> behaviors that increase follow-through and employee commitment.

Notice the underlined words in the example. They are actionable and clearly describe the targeted goals. This makes it easier to determine the necessary content for your training and easier to measure results once the learning experiences have been completed (because you know what behaviors, changes, and improvements to look for).

The Learning Objective describes what learning(s) will take place at the end of the training experience - identifying the outcomes of the training event. It identifies what the participant(s) will gain in knowledge, ability, and/or values. Less detailed than the Program Objective (because the scope is smaller), the Learning Objective is written primarily for the participant and instructor.

> **Ex 4.2 Learning Objective**
>
> At the end of this course, participants will be able to <u>identify</u> opportunities to coach employees for performance improvement; <u>apply</u> the 5 steps of effective coaching in both real and simulated instances; <u>utilize</u> appropriate feedback tools when giving praise and /or correction; <u>recognize</u> and <u>identify</u> behavior differences through observation; and <u>demonstrate</u> the ability to manage direct reports based on style needs and characteristics.

A Training Objective for a Lesson Plan describes what content and/or information needs to be communicated and taught during the session. It identifies what the instructor needs to accomplish. The Training Objective and lesson plan is written for the trainer / instructor. This is a less common definition of the Training Objective, and is primarily used for teaching "school."

Note: I realize that in many cases, the terms Program Objectives, Learning Objectives, and Training Objectives are used synonymously. I am separating and defining them here for the sake of clarity. My hope is that you will be able to write more effective and comprehensive objectives for your training (in any format) because of an increased understanding of how they should be constructed, and with the right audience in mind.

Criteria for Creating Learning Objectives

Now that the differences in training objectives have been identified, let's look at how one is constructed. You've read the examples, but let's break-down the details. The most common need is for writing the <u>Learning Objective</u>, so this will be the focus of the remainder of this chapter.

As with any blueprint, the layout must be clear and to standard specificity in order for a contractor to build a structure to expectation-level. Likewise, learning objectives have standard criteria that must be met in order for them to be effective. There are three:

- They must be <u>Specific and Clear</u>

    o Describe exactly what the participant will be able to do, think, or feel differently

    o Use words that others can easily understand

    o Describe the conditions in which the participants will be performing (e.g. in a simulation exercise; using standard operating procedures; while being timed; using MS Excel, etc.)

- They must be <u>Results-Orientated</u>

    o Describe the outcome using *action* verbs that identify how the participant will be able to <u>demonstrate</u> their knowledge and skill

    ▪ Words such as understand, learn, and know are not actionable and are therefore inappropriate as objective descriptors (see Ex 4.4-4.6)

    o Identify the specific outcomes *not* the experience (what they will do during the training)

- They must be <u>Measurable</u>

    o Describe the extent / level of competency the participant is expected to achieve

Three Steps to Creating a Learning Objective

Again, objectives talk about the performance of the learners rather than the instructor; they do not describe the textbook, or kinds of classroom experience. They *will*, however, identify the performance, the conditions under which the student will be performing, and provide information concerning the level of performance that will be considered acceptable. (You will notice that the steps are similar to the criteria.)

1. ***Identify the Performance.*** After the training session, the learner will have acquired new skills, knowledge, and/or attitudes. What will they be? Remember the first question the objective answers? "What will participants be able to do, think, or feel differently as a result of the training?" This is where it is answered. Following are the details that describe the three areas of performance:

    - Psychomotor and Behavioral skills, which identify the observable and physical abilities acquired; this includes physical movement, coordination, and use of the motor-skill areas. The development of these skills requires practice and is measured in terms of speed, precision, distance, procedures, or techniques in execution. **(DO)**

    - Cognitive skills, which identify the level of knowledge and intellectual skills gained **(THINK)**

    - Affective competencies, which identify the degree and manner in which participants are able to deal with things emotionally, such as feelings, values, appreciation, enthusiasms, motivations, and attitudes **(FEEL)**

    The key is to use **ACTION** verbs (see Ex 4.4 - 4.6 for examples)

2. ***Identify the Conditions.*** In other words, identify the circumstances in which the learner will be able to perform the task. This is the component that is often missed. Whether it's because the information is less valuable to the participant and/or instructor, because it's more difficult to write, or because the instructor wants more flexibility in creating the learning conditions in the moment, I don't know. However when written correctly, identifying the conditions provide a cleaner, clearer understanding of the planned outcomes. (see Ex 4.2)

3. ***Identify the Level of Acceptance.*** Here you want to identify the specific level of proficiency, quality, or speed of accuracy, error margin, productivity level, degree of excellence, etc. as it pertains to the training content. This answers "How well will the participant be able to perform?" This works best for psychomotor and cognitive skill objectives.

Bloom's Taxonomy[4] of Learning Outcomes

Your best resource for identifying specific performance outcomes is Bloom's Taxonomy. Professor Benjamin Bloom of Chicago University headed a group of educational psychologists from 1948 to 1956, and together they developed a classification of levels of thinking behaviors and attitudinal abilities thought to be important in the process of learning. This became a taxonomy that included the three domains[6]: cognitive (knowledge-based), psychomotor / kinesthetic (physical and perceptual-based), and affective (value-based).

From the cognitive domain, Bloom devised a "stairway" (exhibit 4.3) with six major steps to learning - each building upon the other - beginning with the lowest conceptual level to the conceptually complex. Bloom has divided knowledge into a hierarchical scheme, the components of which become essential parts of objectives, teaching methods, and assessments.

Ex4.3

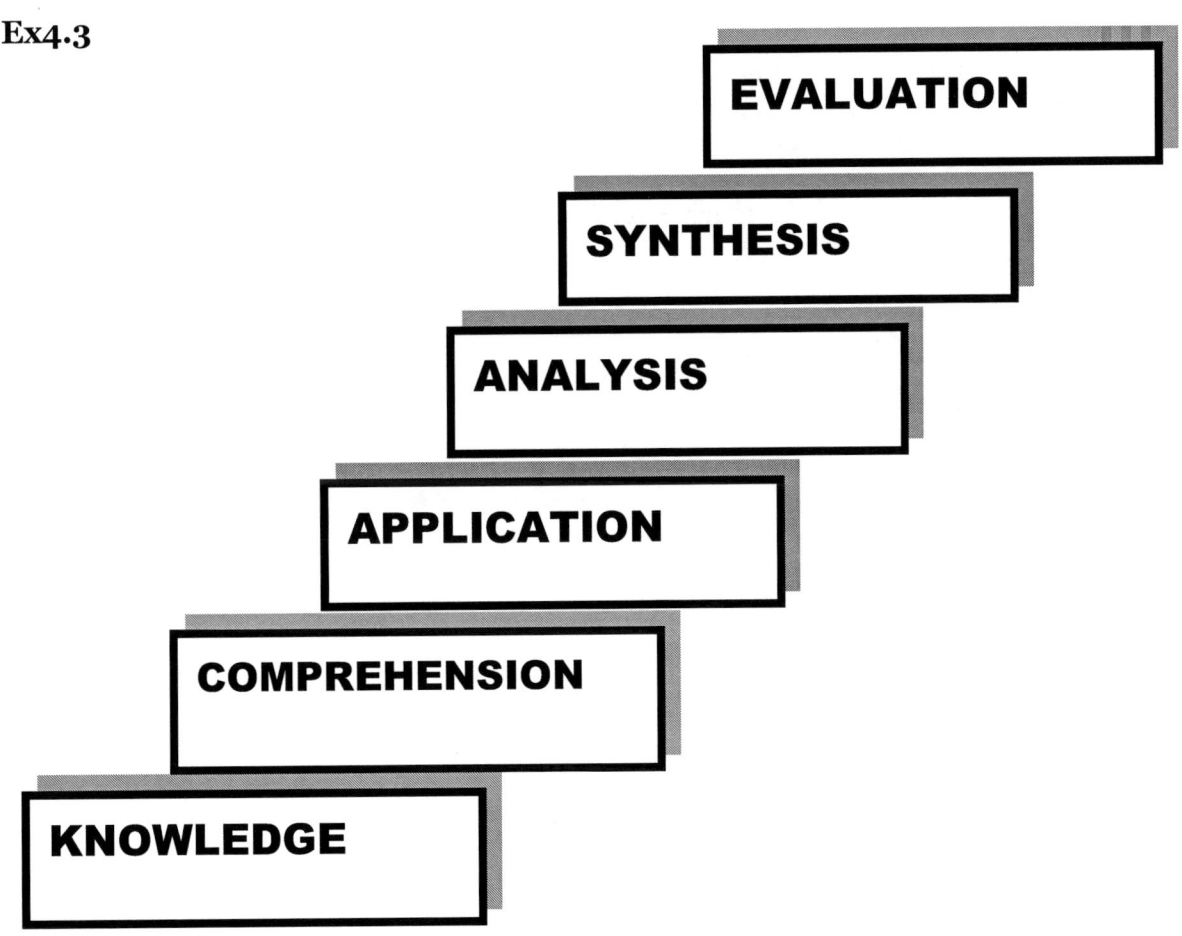

[4] *Taxonomy: The Science of classification*

[5] *Domain: a realm or range of personal knowledge, responsibility, etc.*

Bloom's[6] cognitive (knowledge-based) levels from low to high, with appropriate verbs for objective outcomes, are defined in the table below:

Ex 4.4 Cognitive Levels (lowest to highest)

Competence Level	**Skill**	**Actionable Verbs**
Knowledge	Recall information; know major ideas	Identify, define, translate, tell, quote, name, show, memorize, list, record
Comprehension	Understand information; grasp meaning; interpret facts; group	Explain, describe, interpret, contrast, predict, associate, differentiate, distinguish, summarize, locate
Application	Use information; use methods in new situations; solve problems	Apply, demonstrate, complete, illustrate, examine, modify, relate, classify, discover, change, translate, use, operate
Analysis	Pull information apart and re-establish; see patterns; organize the parts; identify components	Analyze, separate, connect, classify, arrange, divide, compare, select, infer, appraise, calculate, test, diagram
Synthesis	Simplify and make clear; use old ideas to create new ones; generalize from given facts; draw conclusions	Integrate, modify, rearrange, substitute, create, design, formulate, rewrite, plan, invent, assemble, manage, prepare, propose
Evaluation	Assess and make judgments; discriminate between ideas; make choices based on argument; verify value of evidence	Assess, decide, rank, measure, recommend, convince, judge, discriminate, conclude, compare, score, estimate, value

[6] *The most useful reference for trainers is Bloom's work:* <u>Taxonomy of Educational Objectives: Cognitive Domain.</u>

4.5 Affective Levels (lowest to highest)

Competence Level	Skill	Actionable Verbs
Receiving Information or Experiences	Awareness, willingness to hear, selected attention.	Asks, chooses, describes, follows, gives, holds, identifies, locates, names, points to, selects, sits, erects, replies, uses.
Responding to Information and Experiences	Active participation on the part of the learners; reacts. Learning outcomes may emphasize compliance in responding, willingness to respond, or satisfaction in responding (motivation).	Answers, assists, aids, complies, conforms, discusses, greets, helps, labels, performs, practices, presents, reads, recites, reports, selects, tells, writes.
Valuing	The worth or value a person attaches to a particular object, experience, or behavior. Valuing is based on the internalization of a set of specified values, while clues to these values are expressed in the learner's overt behavior and are often identifiable.	Completes, demonstrates, differentiates, explains, follows, forms, initiates, invites, joins, justifies, proposes, reads, reports, selects, shares, studies, works.
Organization	Organizes values into priorities by contrasting different values, resolving conflicts between them, and creating a unique value system.	Adheres, alters, arranges, combines, compares, completes, defends, explains, formulates, generalizes, identifies, integrates, modifies, orders, organizes, prepares, relates, synthesizes.
Internalizing values (characterization)	Has a value system that controls their behavior. The behavior is pervasive, consistent, predictable, and most importantly, characteristic of the learner.	Acts, discriminates, displays, influences, listens, modifies, performs, practices, proposes, qualifies, questions, revises, serves, solves, verifies.

4.6 Psychomotor / Kinesthetic Levels (lowest to highest)

Competence Level	Skill	Actionable Verbs
Perception	The ability to use sensory cues to guide motor activity. This ranges from sensory stimulation, through cue selection, to translation.	Chooses, describes, detects, differentiates, distinguishes, identifies, isolates, relates, selects.
Set	Readiness to act. It includes mental, physical, and emotional sets. (sometimes called mindsets).	Begins, displays, explains, moves, proceeds, reacts, shows, states, volunteers.
Guided Response	The early stages in learning a complex skill that includes imitation and trial and error.	Copies, traces, follows, react, reproduce, responds
Mechanism	This is the intermediate stage in learning a complex skill. Learned responses have become habitual and the movements can be performed with some confidence and proficiency.	Assembles, calibrates, constructs, dismantles, displays, fastens, fixes, grinds, heats, manipulates, measures, mends, mixes, organizes, sketches.
Complex Overt Response	The skillful performance of motor acts that involve complex movement patterns. Proficiency is indicated by a quick, accurate, and highly coordinated performance, requiring a minimum of energy. This category includes performing without hesitation, and automatic performance.	The Key Words are the same as Mechanism, but will have adverbs or adjectives that indicate that the performance is quicker, better, more accurate, etc.
Adaptation	Skills are well developed and the individual can modify movement patterns to fit special requirements.	Adapts, alters, changes, rearranges, reorganizes, revises, varies.
Origination	Creates new movement patterns to fit a particular situation or specific problem. Learning outcomes emphasize creativity based upon highly developed skills.	Arranges, builds, combines, composes, constructs, creates, designs, initiate, makes, originates.

Review Quiz

Matching

_____ 1. Program Objective

a) Describes what content and/or information needs to be communicated and taught during the session. It identifies what the instructor needs to accomplish.

_____ 2. Learning Objective

b) Describes what learning(s) will take place at the end of the training experience - identifying the outcomes of the training event; written primarily for the participant and instructor.

_____ 3. Training Objective for Lesson Plans

c) Addresses the issues/problems uncovered in the needs assessment. It describes what will be different after *all* courses have been completed: what will be different for the participant, different for the organization, and different in terms of solving the "problem;" is written primarily for the instructor and the company /or training stakeholders.

4. A learning objective describes the process towards the means, and is written from the instructor's perspective. True or False? _____

5. List the four criteria standards that an objective must meet in order to be effective.

    1) _____

    2) _____

    3) _____

    4) _____

6. What three steps to creating an objective?

    1) _____

    2) _____

    3) _____

7. Benjamin Bloom devised a "stairway" with six major steps of learning in the cognitive domain. What will participants be able to do if they are taught to the lowest level of cognitive understanding?

_____

_____

8. What will participants be able to do if they are taught to the highest level of cognitive understanding?

_____

_____

9. Write a simple learning objective with a learning level of "Analysis" based on Bloom's Cognitive domain.

_____

_____

_____.

10. Write a simple learning objective with a learning level of "Valuing" based on Bloom's Affective Domain.

_____

_____

_____.

1.c; 2a; . 3b; 4. False; 5.Specific and clear, Results-orientated, Measurable; 6. Performance, Condition, Level of acceptance; 7. They will be able to recall information and know major ideas; 8. They will be able to assess and make judgments, and discriminate between ideas.

Tool Five: The Training Plan

Planning what training to deliver, to whom, and to what extent is similar to planning and structuring a presentation. First determine your outcomes, then identify the content that will get you and your audience where you want to go, prioritize the content and map out a logical flow of delivery (sequencing), select the most effective delivery methods for the audience and topic, then prepare, practice, and deliver.

Ask yourself these questions:

- What must the learners / class participants be able to do, think, or feel differently after their training has been completed?

- What content, experiences, and resources will help them achieve this outcome?

- What tools are already available?

- What are the barriers, if any?

- How long will it take?

- How much will it cost?

- What are the most effective delivery formats?

- Who can best deliver the training, and where?

- How will you know the training was successful?

DIFFERENT PLANS FOR DIFFERENT STRUCTURES

After answering the questions above, you could begin writing a plan for a curriculum, a program, an individual course or a lesson plan. In one sense, they are *all* training plans, true: the phrase "training plan" has been the generic term for all plans that have to do with training.

For this study, however, I will differentiate the plans for the sake of clarity. One thing I learned early in my career was to make sure I understood the definitions of terms and lingo. If I didn't, I would assume an expectation that often was wrong, or create an outcome different than what was needed.

A Curriculum includes several courses within a related topic or subject matter that are connected by a global objective. This term is more often used to describe a field of study offered by an educational institution, but can be used in the business or corporate setting.

Example: An *engineering curriculum* - is *for* engineers and/or will *produce* engineers *(university)*; a *Leadership Curriculum* – is *for* leaders and/or will *produce* leaders (corporate training)

A Program is very similar to a curriculum in the sense that it includes several courses, but the program is specific to the skill, such as a computer training program, or communications program. Again, there may be several courses within the program but they're all related to the skill set.

Example: The computer training program will provide all courses necessary for an individual to use the computer at a mastery level; the communications training program will include several courses to make an individual a more effective communicator.

Note: in the corporate world, the term "training program" is often used synonymously with "curriculum."

A Course is a single topic or subject of instruction or study, such as an interviewing course. Participants learn one focused skill / knowledge set.

Example: The interviewing course will provide the information and tools to conduct an effective interview. It won't cover any other HR or management practices that do not pertain to interviewing.

A Lesson Plan, is a roadmap for the trainer / facilitator that describes in detail <u>how</u> to conduct the class session; it is, in effect, the facilitator's manual. Although the lesson plan includes training outcomes (usually what will be covered in the session), it is written *for* the instructor, not the participant.

Example: The lesson plan will identify what materials are needed and tell the facilitator what to say and when, provide what questions to ask after an exercise, identify what visuals to use, and the instructions for conducting activities.

FOUR TYPES OF LEARNING PROGRAM FORMATS

Although we often use the terms "training," and "training program" to generically include all types of learning opportunities and formats, there are four different learning program formats with distinct differences in the definitions and intent of each. The four program formats are: **training, development, education, and awareness.**

A training program is different from a development program in that ***training*** is a process of gaining "task-focused" skills for the immediate present, and ***development*** is focused on growth and future preparation. The very nature of these differences suggests very different program expectations and outcomes:

- At the end of a training program, participants will be able to <u>do</u> something they were not previously able to do.

- At the end of a development program, participants will be able to <u>assume higher levels of responsibility</u> that they were not able to take-on previously.

Similarly, an educational program is different from an awareness program. ***Education*** is a long-term process of informational and learning opportunities that provide diverse perspectives on various subject matters within a general "family of knowledge," and stimulates creativity. ***Awareness*** is a "subject-focused" learning that is often attitudinal (addressing attitudes, feelings, and values) and leads one to make knowledgeable choices.

- At the end of an educational program, participants will be able <u>to "Think outside the box," and champion change.</u>

- At the end of an awareness program, participants will be able to <u>make knowledgeable choices of behavior and/or action.</u>

> *In this chapter, the "Training Plan" refers to a plan for either a curriculum or program. The "How-tos" can be applied to any of the above learning formats: training, development, education, or awareness.*

STEPS TO CREATING A TRAINING PLAN

In its first stage, the instructional plan is an opportunity to organize one's thoughts and rationale, and to clearly identify the desired outcomes. Ultimately, your training plan will specifically describe these outcomes in the form of *objectives*, and identify the sequential content, the methodology, and the measurement (results indicator).

There are five basic steps to creating an effective training plan:

1. **Determine Program Objectives / Outcomes**[1]

    a. What has the greatest value to "stakeholders?"[2]

    b. What is "Do-able" and Realistic?

2. **Determine the Appropriate Content (What do participants need to be taught?)**

    a. What information, skills, or experiences need to be provided to successfully meet your objectives?

    b. What learning will fill the knowledge gap and solve potential problems for the participants and the organization?

    c. What skills, knowledge, and experiences are within your means to provide (either internally or by outsourcing)?

3. **Sequence Skills by Type & Level**

    a. Determine the level of skill / knowledge competency participants need to achieve in order to meet objectives

    b. Consider Bloom's[3] level of learning

    c. Take participants through ja logical flow of information that uses what they already have learned to help them assimilate new information (Move content from known to unknown) [4]

---

[1] *Remember the objectives for a training plan are <u>different</u> from learning objectives in that they are broader in scope and describe the targeted outcomes of the entire program, they describe the bigger picture. (See chapter 4) j*

[2] *We talk about stakeholders in chapter 2 when conducting a needs assessment. Again, these are primarily the individuals who serve to gain or lose based on the outcomes of your training program. They may also be the ones who asked for the training, or are funding the training.*

[3] *Benjamin Bloom's Taxonomy of Learning; review exhibit 4.3*

[4] *This is called "Velcro Learning." The reason it is called this is because this strategy helps the content "stick" in the minds of the participants.*

4. **Determine Methodology (Delivery Format)**

    a. How will you deliver the content?

5. **Determine Results Indicator**

    a. How will you know you have succeeded?

    b. What measurements will you use?

Determine Program Objectives. Once again, this is different from a learning objective which identifies (from the learner's perspective) what will be different in their understanding and/or ability at the end of the learning experience. When you formulate <u>this </u>objective, it is from a global perspective that meets the organizational or stakeholder's needs. What will this training provide back to the company? What problem(s) will it solve? How will the organization benefit?

The Program Objective articulates the "desired state" of your program. It provides the "Who" (the learning audience), the "What" (what will be different), and the "Benefit(s)." (See example 5.1 below)

Ex 5.1

At the completion of this program, mid-level managers will be able to: Transition from managing "things" and processes to leading organizational change; promote and inspire behaviors that support and maintain a culture of inclusion and teamwork; increase quality and performance results within their business units to "standard" or above; and coach and develop high potential employees to enhance succession planning efforts.

Determine Content. The most important factor in determining content is to identify what the participants "need-to-know" versus what would be "nice-to-know." If you have completed an occupational analysis and scope and sequence (chapter 3), the content can be extrapolated from your prioritized skill and competency list. Another source of content is your interview notes from your initial needs assessment. <u>Make sure, however, that your content decisions are in sync with your objectives</u> / outcomes, including the learning points within each content component.

Using example 5.1, your content may consist of the following:

- Managing Change
- Leading vs. Managing
- Managing Diversity
- Team Leadership
- Communication Skills
- Setting Performance Expectations
- Mentoring and Coaching Skills
- Influencing Skills

Once the "what" of your content has been determined, you may choose to write your own courses utilizing subject-matter-experts, or purchase them from a training development vendor. (See list of possible vendors in References and Resources section.) Do your homework: research the topics and who the experts are; read books and articles that have been written within the pervious five years; brainstorm with subject-matter-experts; collect data and prioritize based on the "need-to-know" rule.

Sequence Skills. The next step in your planning process is arranging the content in a logical order. Remember to build knowledge upon knowledge and lead the participant from known-to-unknown, which we previously described as "Velcro Learning." For example, if you are designing a customer service program, you may have determined that the participants need *telephone service skills, understanding behavior, dealing with difficult cus*tomers, and *service standards*. Moving from a logical flow of known to unknown, or simple to complex, you may arrange the topics in the following sequential order:

a) Service Standards

b) Understanding Behavior

c) Telephone Service Skills

d) Dealing with Difficult Customers

One technique you may want to use is "storyboarding." This is a technique used by detectives (you may have seen this on television's "Law and Order," "CSI," or "Missing") in order to unravel a case. Each piece of information is put on a separate piece of paper, and then posted on a wall or window in different arrangements until the most logical flow is discovered. One easy way to storyboard content is to put each topic on a "sticky-note" and continue to move them around until the flow makes sense.

Storyboarding Ex 5.2

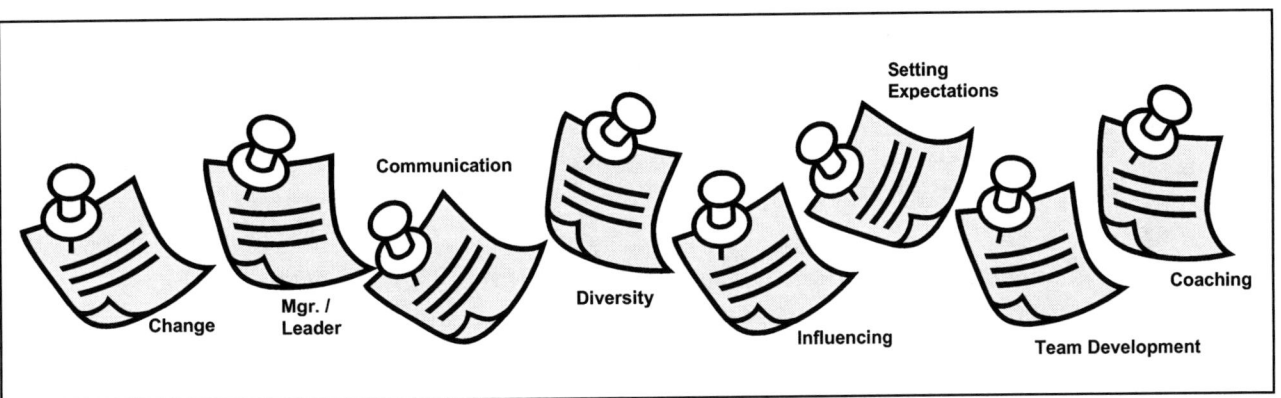

Your goal in sequencing is to maximize learning. Whether the order represents a step-by-step process of "need-to-know" or an order based on priority of information, keep the learner's need to retain the information and value the experience foremost in your design.

Determine Methodology (Delivery Format). Lois Hart[5] in her handbook for trainers calls training delivery formats the "meat on the bones" and "frosting on the cake" of your training program design. They add variety, creativity, and interest to your training. Using a multiplicity of formats (methods) in your delivery will also satisfy the diversity of learning styles, personality, and knowledge-level of your audience.

[5]*Lois Hart, Training Methods that Work; Crisp Publications*

An entire chapter is devoted to instructional methods (Instructional Methods and Materials page 53), however some of the most common are listed here:

- **Classroom presentation style (lecturette):** trainer tells

- **Discussions:** participants share knowledge and opinions while trainer guides / facilitates

- **Role play:** participants practice skills by "acting out" scenarios

- **Worksheets and manuals**: participants write, list, and capture information on paper

- **Web-based**: participants learning via the internet / intranet; this may be facilitator led or independent study

- **Videos:** participants experience a "show and tell" illustration for the models and skills you are teaching, via professional actors and/or presenters

Determine Results Indicator. Once you have planned and delivered your training, you need to know if the information was understood and retained to the level of your expectations and intent, and that your program objectives have been reached. At the end of the learning experience, many trainers will use the "smile sheet" - a questionnaire that solicits reactions and input of usability from participants - but often only discover whether the participants "enjoyed" it or not.

A results indicator is a measurement tool used to gauge the degree of improvement or change following the training. It answers the question: "Was the training effective, and if so, to what extent?" One thing to keep in mind is the primary objective for the session. If it was to reduce the error rate of invoicing, then reviewing the error rate a few weeks post-training would be the appropriate result indicator.

Following are a few additional Results Indicators:

- **Pre-post Surveys:** participants / audience is surveyed before and after the training to measure change in perception

- **Skills Assessments:** an individual's skill level is assessed based on his /her own perception and the perception(s) of his/her manager and compared to others performing the same tasks

- **Measurable Increase in Output:** participants / attendees performance is quantitative and is measured before and after training to determine level of improvement

- **Employee Surveys:** the culture of an organization is assessed through the eyes of its employees; training is one component that is asked about and examined

- **Certification Tests:** usually a written test given to determine competency to job standards

- **Demonstrations:** participants are able to show evidence of their skills by performing tasks in front of the instructor for evaluation

> The best time to determine the most appropriate indicator is during the planning process. As you identify your objectives, identify how you will determine your success. When you decide on content, decide on how you will "test for understanding" after the content has been presented.

Putting it all Together

Exhibit 5.3 is an example of a training plan drafted from the Occupational Analysis and Scope and Sequence analysis of the Training Manager (chapter 3). It combines all elements: objectives, contents in sequence, level of learning (Bloom), method(s), and results indicator.

Ex 5.3

TRAINING PLAN WORKSHEET (From Occupational Analysis – Chapter 3)

Job / Position: Corporate Training Manager

Program Objective: Training Mangers will be able to function as business partners to the organization and master facilitators for subject-matter-experts and novice trainers.

Prerequisites: Mastery of facilitation skills and training methods; leadership ability

COMPETENCY/ SKILL	LEARNING OBJECTIVE	COGNITIVE OUTCOMES (from Blooms)	LEVEL / SEQUENCE	FORMAT(s)	ASSESSMENT/ RESULTS INDICATOR
Time Management	To utilize time management tools to organize and prioritize tasks for time efficiency.	Application	Basic/1	Workbooks; computer-based instruction	Written responses to computer program scenarios
HR Law and Compliance	To be familiar with minimum law requirements for managing workforce and how they apply	Comprehension	Basic/2	Video; discussion	Oral quiz
Managing Diversity	To increase sensitivity to differences and integrate knowledge of diversity dimensions with effective management practices	Application	Inter./1	Lecturette; exercises; worksheets; discussion	Employee surveys; reduced litigation
Conflict Resolution	To determine root causes of conflict and create win/win resolve	Analysis	Inter./2	Lecturette; exercises; worksheets; role play	Demonstration through role plays
Developing Trainers	To be able to cultivate talent, motivate, and increase skills of novice trainers	Synthesis	Mstr /1	Workshop /clinic	Train-back
Problem Solving and Decision Making	To analyze complex issues and utilize system thinking tools for making decisions	Evaluation	Mstr /2	Lecturette; Video; Discussion; Role play;	Written analysis & proposal from case study
Instructional Design and Development	To create effective training / development plans for corporate curriculum and workshops	Synthesis	Mstr /3	Lecturette; worksheets; skill practice	Demonstration with written designs
Internal Consulting	To assess needs, analyze performance problems, measure ROI, and recommend un-biased solutions	Evaluation	Mstr /4	Lecturette; Discussion; Case study; Assessment instruments	Demonstration through role plays and case study analysis

FOLLOW THROUGH

Your responsibilities are not over after the design and development of your training program. From here, you must prepare and support the instructors, oversee the scheduling and classroom logistics, prepare materials, and conduct the internal marketing. You want to ensure that the program you designed on paper is just as effective in its execution.

Another success factor that is often overlooked is anticipating the answer to the "What next?" question. How will you ensure that your participants apply what they've learned? Training doesn't stop even after the session is over. How participants will transfer their learning back on the job must be written into the training design. You certainly want participants to gain knowledge, but greater still, you want them to retain it and use it.

Tips:

1. Set action plans with participants *during* the training session

2. Solicit feedback from managers, trainers, and participants throughout the training process in order to make adjustments and improvements that will enhance application.

3. Coach and motivate the managers of the participants before the training. He/she may recommend follow-though activities for on-the-job reinforcement, and help identify barriers that block the application of new skills.

4. Keep a record of your training project with all your development resources – key information, costs, and assessment results – to use as a framework for future projects, and as a learning tool for other trainers/developers.

5. Schedule a post-training session with all the individuals involved in the development

    o Document the experience as well as the process

    o Identify what worked and what did not

    o Provide an opportunity for everyone to acknowledge the contributions of other team mates

Review Quiz

1. Name the five major steps of creating an effective training plan:

    1) _____

    2) _____

    3) _____

    4) _____

    5) _____

2. What is the difference between a training program and a development program?

    _____

    _____.

3. What happens in the sequencing process of creating a training plan?

    _____.

4. What will participants be able to do after an educational program?

    _____.

5. A results indicator is a measurement tool used to gauge the degree of change after the training experience. True or False? _____

6. When is the best time to determine the most appropriate results indicator?

    _____.

7. List two examples of a results indicator:

    1) _____

    2) _____

8. What is the one success factor that is often overlooked?

    _____.

Matching

_____ 9. A Curriculum

a) A roadmap for the trainer / facilitator that describes in detail <u>how</u> to conduct the class session; it is, in effect, the facilitator's manual. It is written *for* the instructor, not the participant.

_____ 10. A Lesson Plan

b) A single topic or subject of instruction or study. Participants learn one focused skill / knowledge set.

_____ 11. A Training Program

c) Several courses within a related topic or subject matter that are connected by a global objective. This term is more often used to describe a field of study offered by an educational institution, but can be used in the business or corporate setting.

_____ 12. A Course

d) Several courses collected together that are specific to a skill. Again, there may be several courses within, but they're all related to the skill set.

---

1. Determine objectives, Determine content, Sequence skills, Determine methods, Determine results indicator; 2. A training program is a process of gaining task-focused skills for immediate use, a development program is focused on growth and future preparation; 3. The content is arranged in a logical order; 4. Think outside the box and champion change; 5. True; 6. During the planning process; 7. Any of the following: Surveys, Skill Assessments, Measurable increases, Tests, Demonstrations; 8. Anticipating the answer to "what's next?" 9. c; 10.a; 11. d; 12 b

Personal Notes

Tool Six: Instructional Methods and Materials

Conducting a needs assessment and determining your program objectives help to identify the "what" of your training plan. The methods or formats you choose to deliver your content constitute the "how." *How* will you motivate the adult learners in your session? *How* will you meet their diverse stylistic needs for learning and retaining information? *How* will you keep your audience engaged? *How* will you develop personal responsibility for learning in your participants?

The "hows" go on, but the answer's the same: by using a variety of training methods as a vehicle to effectively carry your content and guide the participants through the discovery and learning process.

When selecting training methods, consider your objectives and what will best accomplish your goal(s). One method is not necessarily better than another, but there are a few considerations you need to keep in mind:

- What is most appropriate for the content / subject?

- How much time do you have? (allow equal time for participants to complete an activity and for you to facilitate the processing of the experience)

- How large is your group?

- Where are your participants located? Local? Nationwide? International?

- What equipment is needed?

- How comfortable are you with the format?

- What is the level of risk for participants?

- Are there combinations that would work well together? (e.g.: a video followed by group discussion; a demonstration with train-back)

E-learning options have become increasingly prevalent for virtual teams and international, and cross-continental employees. According to the latest research from ASTD (American Society for Training and Development) however, the classroom still remains the primary format for training and development, especially for non-technical training.

The following pages describe several instructional methods that can be used to creatively deliver content in a classroom setting. Many of the methods are forms of active - or cooperative - learning techniques. Based on recent research at the college level, students who actively engage with the material are more likely to recall information later and be able to use that information in different contexts (Bruner, 1961).

Active learning is an umbrella term that refers to several models of instruction that focus the responsibility of learning, on learners. Bonwell and Eison (1991) popularized this approach to instruction. This "buzz word" of the 1980s, became their 1990s report to the Association for the Study of Higher Education (ASHE). In this report they discuss a variety of methodologies for promoting "active learning." This strategy assumes that the learning process is learner driven, but this does not mean that an instructor can dispense guidance. You must provide challenges, encourage risk taking, correct errors, and provide context.

The effectiveness of active instructional techniques like active learning has been questioned in recent years. While it makes sense to use these techniques as a "followup" exercise, it does not make sense to use them to introduce material. It is suggested that you guide your students in the early stages of learning, and later let them practice their new learned skills or apply new information.

Discovery and Inquiry-based Instruction: A teaching technique in which teachers create situations in which students are to solve problems. Lessons are designed so that students make connections to previous knowledge, bring their own questions to learning, investigate to satisfy their own questions and design ways to try out their ideas. Such investigations may extend over a long period of time. Students communicate through journal writing, oral presentations, drawing, graphing, charting, etc. Students then revise their explanations as they learn.

This technique is particularly popular in science instruction. Discovery learning is a type of inquiry-based instruction which was developed primarily by the psychologist Jerome Bruner.

The inquiry-based instruction approach has been most widely used in science education, but it has also been used in a number of other subject matter areas including mathematics, engineering and even reading instruction.

Experienthodic: A type of experiential learning and participatory method of instruction / training that immerses the participant into the learning environment, and systematically leads them to a knowledge or understanding by way of experience.

The participant is actively involved in the process as well as the learning during the experience, even to the extent that the experience *itself* provides the knowledge.

This method utilizes "senses" as learning tools: sound, emotion, touch, feel, sight, taste, and smell. The discovery method's success relies on the exercises that lead to the unexpected. It should represent the content in a way that places them in a real-world situation, but is simple enough that all can participate.

Example:

Participants learn the destructive impact of discrimination by being put into a situation where they are excluded, shunned, and otherwise given unfair treatment because of a characteristic which they may or may not be aware of. By the same token, participants may have their inner biases provoked by the situation an exercise creates, and consequently learn how to recognize and address their issues and resolve internal and external conflicts.

Edutainment: A teaching method/technique that entertains the participant while providing an educational and/or "awareness" message. Participants may or may not be directly involved in the presentation, but are most often represented. This is different from watching films. This method involves active learning as an aspect of the experience.

This format heavily utilizes music, humor, and animations, including creating music parodies that participants themselves sing, improvisations, and other creative expressions.

Demonstration: A teaching technique used for skill-based instruction that systematically "walks" the participant through the steps and actions needed to complete a specific task.

This technique is first used by the instructor and is often followed by a skill-practice from the participant(s), as in teaching by rote.

Skill Practice: A method similar to the demonstration method, but is performed by the participant. He /she repeats a series of steps and processes previously taught by the instructor.

Most often, a Skill Practice will include several skills performed in succession, in order to complete the task / objective.

Train-back: A technique similar to the Skill Practice with one exception: the participant (student) teaches the acquired skill to another participant while being observed / coached by the instructor.

This is an excellent evaluation technique to assess understanding and level of skill attained.

Lecturette: An instructional method/technique performed by the instructor and is used to communicate information by "telling." The lecturette, however is a shortened version of a lecture, and lasts 20 minutes or less, covering one presented topic only. This is about the maximum attention span for most adult learners.

This format is commonly followed by a group discussion covering the presented topic.

Note-taking: A retention method that holds participants accountable for capturing and summarizing the main points of the content. The visual and kinesthetic learner may take notes automatically, while others find it a distraction to listening and learning. Note-taking can be very helpful when the content includes a complicated procedure or several critical steps to a process that is important for participants to remember.

"Fill-in-the-blanks:" A structured note-taking method that is both a tool and technique, giving accountability to the learner for retaining the information, while also keeping them focused by giving them *something to do* during a lecturette.

In this format, the participants fill-in missing details in a handout that outlines the content.

Discussion: A learner-focused technique used to share ideas, views, and individual / group understanding of a topic.

This format draws on the knowledge and experience of the participants, and is particularly motivating to the oratory learner (the interpersonal-verbal style). This method may be used in small groups, pairs, and with full classroom participation. A common technique is to have participants think about an issue, share it with a partner or in small groups, then collectively provide feedback to the whole class (think, pair, share).

Role Play: With this method, participants "act-out" scenarios in a low-risk environment.

Participants are able to obtain feedback and insight on their behavior / actions.

Simulations: A complex experienthodic method that imitates real life situations for the participant. This is an excellent way to integrate several new skills, and provide an opportunity for participants to affect the situation without risk.

Case Study: A discovery format where participants practice problem-solving skills by studying a situation that causes them to utilize the new knowledge in a risk free environment. This format works well when combined with group discussions.

Games: A method that integrates fun and competition into the learning experience, and promotes "active learning." Games stimulate the kinesthetic and interpersonal /oratory learner, and helps to improve retention, but is time consuming and more difficult for the instructor to control.

The Fish Bowl: Another discussion method, but with a smaller group forming an "inner-circle" to talk and share ideas, while the other participants listen and observe. This works particularly well when those in the fishbowl (the inner circle) are subject-matter-experts, and other participants are able to ask questions at the end of the discussion.

Warm-ups and Icebreakers: An activity designed to get the participants involved right a way and set a positive tone for the learning environment. They are also used to increase the energy of the group and provide a fun way to introduce the topic.

Storytelling: This can be a powerful technique, yet it is so often overlooked. People love to hear real-life accounts, especially if they contain humor, and it is an interesting way to illustrate major points of the content.

Using the story to illustrate examples can add credibility to your training by making it "real." Stories and analogies can also help participants "relate" to the material by adding the element of human emotions to the presentation.

Assessments and Personal Inventories: A paper-and-pencil method of information gathering providing a snap-shot measurement of the participant's behavior and/or skill level pertaining to the learning content.

This method is useful in creating a baseline for future individual growth, but should be used with sensitivity with those participants who see it as threatening, and are fearful of stereotyping. Explain to participants why you chose this instrument and the "WIIFM" (what's in it for me – in this case, *them*). Point out also that there are no right or wrong answers.

After completing the instrument, you may want to engage participants in an activity that reinforces the theory behind the topic, or present a lecturette that will do the same.

Blended Learning: The combination of multiple approaches to learning. Blended learning can be accomplished through the use of 'blended' virtual and physical resources. A typical example of this would be a combination of technology-based materials and face-to-face sessions used together to deliver instruction.

In the strictest sense, blended learning is anytime any instructor combines two or more methods of delivery of instruction. However, the deeper meaning lies in engaging the students of the current generation. Thus a better example would be using active learning techniques in the physical classroom and a web presence online.

With today's prevalence of high technology in many countries, blended learning often refers specifically to the provision or use of resources which combine e-learning (electronic) or m-learning (mobile) with other educational resources.

DELIVERY TIPS:

- When selecting materials, make sure that videos, DVDs, case studies, illustrations, etc. represent a culturally diverse audience.

- Know as much as you can about your participants in advance, and prepare for any disabilities, including hearing, vision, literacy, and learning disabilities. Create materials at an appropriate reading level, and large enough for more senior participants to see.

- When there is a language barrier, don't assume a nod means agreement or understanding. Ask open-ended questions or look for demonstrations of comprehension.

- Consider that smiles and laughter may be a sign of discomfort or embarrassment. Read your audience and try to identify the real cause when there's confusion.

- Be careful in using first names, especially with older participants. Ask people what they prefer to be called.

- Draw cues from non-verbal communication.

- Create opportunities for participants to learn about each other in structured activities.

- Ask participants for correct pronunciation of their name, and practice saying them.

- Avoid gender-specific language in materials.

- Be careful with humor. Watch for cultural cues that will tell you when it is acceptable or not.

MATERIALS

The materials a trainer uses for content delivery include handouts, worksheets, assessment instruments, instructions for activities and games, visual aids, CD and DVD applications, instructor manuals, etc. These materials are also part of the trainers' "toolkit;" they are the instruments that create the experiential impact of the learning symphony.

For classroom instruction, materials fall into two categories: participant guide / information and instructor tools. The participant guide is a packaged set of information that will be used in class and as an on-the-job reference for the learner. It includes all the materials needed to complete the course, a copy of the visuals, relevant articles, informational pages, and materials needed to complete activities.

The instructor tools include an amplified version of the participant guide, lecture notes, instructions for activity set-up and implementation, visuals, and notes to guide classroom discussions.

Creating these instruments is very time consuming, so keep the objectives and the audience in mind. Adults have high expectations for the content and the materials they receive to guide them through the content. They should be high quality, professionally appealing, and easy to navigate.

Make sure to include:

- Clear headings
- Short paragraphs
- Easily read fonts
- Space for taking notes
- Relevant graphics and illustrations
- Summary checklists
- Examples and exercises

Review Quiz

Matching

Match the instructional method with the appropriate definition.

_____ 1. Skill Practice

_____ 2. Role Play

_____ 3. Edutainment

_____ 4. Simulations

_____ 5. Blended Learning

_____ 6. Discovery and Inquiry

_____ 7. Train-back

_____ 8. Storytelling

_____ 9. Case Study

_____ 10. Fishbowl

e) A teaching technique in which teachers create situations in which students are to solve problems.

f) A technique which uses the combination of multiple approaches to learning.

g) A discovery format where participants practice problem-solving skills by studying a situation that causes them to utilize the new knowledge in a risk free environment.

h) Another discussion method, but with a smaller group forming an "inner-circle" to talk and share ideas, while the other participants listen and observe.

i) With this method, participants "act-out" scenarios in a low-risk environment.

j) A complex experienthodic method that imitates real life situations for the participant; an opportunity for participants to affect a situation without risk.

k) A teaching method/technique that entertains the participant while providing an educational and/or "awareness" message.

l) A method similar to the demonstration method, but is performed by the participant. He/she repeats a series of steps and processes previously taught by the instructor.

m) A technique similar to the Skill Practice with one exception: the participant (student) teaches the acquired skill to another participant while being observed / coached by the instructor.

n) A method of using analogies to help participants "relate" to the material by adding the element of human emotions to the presentation.

Review Quiz Continued

11. What must you consider when selecting a training method?
    _____

12. Active learning is an umbrella term for classroom training that is instructor driven with many activities and exercises for the participants to engage in. True or False? _____

13. What are the four most common forms of active learning?

    1) _____

    2) _____

    3) _____

    4) _____

1.h; 2.e; 3.g; 4.f; 5.b; 6.a; 7.i; 8.j; 9.c; 10.d; 11. Consider your objectives and what will best accomplish your goals; 12. False; 13. Discovery learning, Problem-based learning, Experiential learning, and Inquiry-based instruction;

Tool Seven: "Master Mixes"

Years ago in grade school, girls were required to take home economics (cooking and sewing) while boys took "shop" and wood-working. In the cooking session, we learned to make a home-made Bisquick™ called a Master Mix. This Master Mix provided the basics for all kinds of baking endeavors: breads, cakes, pancakes, muffins, pie crust, cookies, and cobblers. All one had to do was add the specific ingredients unique to the product, then add water and stir.

There are formulas for lesson plans that work like Bisquick™: just add contents and deliver. These formulas provide a framework for creating a motivating, active, and supportive environment for adults to learn, and simplifies the design work for the trainer.

The goal is always to motivate learners to find meaning in the content and to retain the information. Adults learn best when they are actively involved in the learning process. This will include exercises, role plays, case studies, games, and group discussions. Adults also want to feel good about the experience, and that it adds value to their jobs, careers, and lives.

On the following pages are three Master Mixes:

- **Skill Development:** Transfer of skills
    - One-to-One

- **Awareness and Educational Development:**[1] Transfer of Knowledge
    - One-to-Many

- **Classroom Skill Development:** Transfer of skills
    - One to Many

Each formula includes an outline of the class structure (what the instructor should do) and the process of delivery from the learner perspective (what the learner *wants* the instructor to do).

[1] *Review the Four Types of Learning Programs, pg 40*

Ex 7.1

MASTER MIX

(Training Bisquick™)

ONE-TO-ONE AND ON-THE-JOB TRAINING ⇨ TRANSFER OF SKILLS TO INDIVIDUALS

INSTRUCTOR'S TRAINING OUTLINE:

    I. Introduction / Assessment of Skill

    II. Overview / Expectation(s)

    III. Link this Skill to Bigger Picture – Why it's Important

    IV. Demonstration & Explanation(s)

    V. Skill Practice with Repeat-Explanations (Train-back)

    VI. Feedback / Praise

WHAT THE LEARNER WANTS THE INSTRUCTOR TO DO
(Spoken by the learner):

    ASK ME

    SHOW & TELL ME (In small Pieces)

    LET _ME_ SHOW & TELL

    EVALUATE & PRAISE ME

Ex 7.2

MASTER MIX

(Training Bisquick™)

CLASSROOM DEVELOPMENTAL / EDUCATION ⇨
TRANSFER OF KNOWLEDGE

INSTRUCTOR'S TRAINING OUTLINE:

I. Activity / Energizer (Optional)

II. Introduction
- Introduce Subject / Concept
- Set Climate
- Link this Knowledge to Bigger Picture – Why it's Important
- Explain WIIFM (What's in it for me?)
- Communicate Outcomes / Expectations

III. Lecturette with Visuals

IV. Discussions / Activity (to re-enforce learning)

V. Assess Understanding

VI. Commitment to Action

WHAT THE LEARNER WANTS THE INSTRUCTOR TO DO
(Spoken by the learner):

ORIENTATE ME

CONVINCE ME

TELL ME

SHOW ME (HOW IT WORKS)

LET ME

MAKE ME ACCOUNTABLE

Ex 7.3

MASTER MIX

(Training Bisquick™)

CLASSROOM TRAINING ⇨ TRANSFER OF SKILLS TO GROUPS

INSTRUCTOR'S TRAINING OUTLINE:

I. Activity / Energizer (Assess your audience skill level)

II. Introduction to Skill

- Set Climate
- Link this Skill to Bigger Picture – Why it's Important
- Explain WIIFM (What's in it for me?)
- Communicate Outcomes / Expectations

III. Lecturette with Demonstration

IV. Skill Practice / Train-back

V. Review

WHAT THE LEARNER WANTS THE INSTRUCTOR TO DO *(Spoken by the learner):*

TELL ME

- Where; Why
- How it Connects with Method(s)
- What

SHOW ME

- Demonstration, Examples, Role Plays, Visuals
- How it's done

LET ME

- Skill Practice
- Exercises /Role Plays

EVALUATE OR TELL ME (AGAIN)

- Feedback
- Remind me of what I now can do

PRAISE ME

Review Quiz

Matching

Match the Master Mix with its process and objective.

_____ 1. Awareness and Educational Development

    o) Ask me
       Show and tell me
       Let me show and tell
       Evaluate and praise me

_____ 2. Classroom Skill Development

    p) A transfer of skills, one-to-one

_____ 3. Individual Skill Development

    q) A transfer of knowledge, one-to-many

_____ 4. One-to-one and OJT Training

    r) Tell me
      Show me
      Let me
      Evaluate or tell me again
      Praise me

_____ 5. Classroom / Educational Development

    s) A transfer of skills, one-to-many

_____ 6. Classroom Training

    t) Orientate me
      Convince me
      Tell me
      Show me how it works
      Let me
      Make me accountable

1. c; 2. e; 3. b; 4. a; 5. f; 6.d

Personal Notes

Tool Eight: Visual Aids

Visuals serve as an illustrated example of the content, and as an outline reminder of the content flow. They play an important role in helping participants retain information, but should never try to replace good training techniques or be used as a script. Experts estimate that individuals retain only 10 -20% of what they hear and 30 – 50% of what they see and hear. There's also an old Chinese proverb that states: "What I hear I forget, what I see I remember, what I do, I understand."

A study by R. Benschofter reports the influence of using sight and sound by these statistics:

Method	Recall in 3 Hours	Recall in 3 Days
Telling – Lectures	70%	10%
Showing – Demonstrations and Visuals	72%	20%
Blend of Telling and Showing	85%	65%

In *The Trainer's Handbook,*[1] Karen Lawson reports on two studies sponsored by the 3M company – one with Wharton School's Applied Research Center and the other with the University of Minnesota's Management Information Systems Research Center. The two studies compared the impact of visuals on business presentations and meetings, with the results once again confirming the belief that visuals *do* increase retention and effectiveness:

- Presenters using computer-generated visuals / overheads were perceived as more polished and professional

- Presenters with visuals came across as better prepared, more persuasive, more credible, and more interesting

- Retention of oral presentations increased by 10% and were over 43% more persuasive

- Presenters using computer-generated visuals were perceived as being more concise, clearer, and more effective in using supportive data

[1] *See References and Resources*

The fact that so many studies result in very similar data leaves little doubt of the power of audiovisuals in training and communication.

Visuals enhance the content by stimulating the participants' senses – using colors, pictures, sound, and animation. They capture the attention of the audience while also making clear the key points of the course in a hierarchy that clarifies the relationship between points.

Depending on personal taste, the type of presentation, and appropriateness to the audience, visuals can span the continuum from very simple, to very dramatic and sophisticated. Remember, however, that visual aids are just that: aids. They are not the entire presentation; they reinforce the main points with images, graphics, and key words, yet do not *drive* the presentation.

Most people are not good listeners, so providing the key learning points sequentially on a visual helps the participant follow the organization of the session, reconnect easily if he/she gets distracted, and places the emphasis when and where the trainer wants it to be.

Slides and Transparencies

Computers have become the preferred method of creating and projecting visuals, therefore slides (often on PowerPoint) are the most common format for visuals in corporate training. Nevertheless, some instructors still favor overhead transparencies because of the "hands-on" feeling (you can write, draw and highlight directly on them while facing the audience) and because of the expense of LCD equipment for projecting computer images.

Whether you prefer transparencies or slides, the bullets on the following pages will provide some guidelines for creating more powerful visuals.

Ex 8.1

Great visuals have big, simple, colorful pictures.	**Rules for Visuals** ➢ Big ➢ Simple ➢ Colorful ➢ Pictures.	**Rules for Visuals** ➢ Big ➢ Simple ➢ Colorful ➢ Pictures.
GOOD	**BETTER**	**BEST**

Guidelines for Visuals

- Visuals must be visible, legible, and clear. Visible is to have all letters and graphics seen from even the back of the room; legible is having the images intelligible; clear means that participants can decipher the message on the first read - use fonts at 18-points or more

- Keep it simple; put one idea on a slide with no more than one illustration per slide

- Limit titles / headings to five words or less

- Less is more: there should be only six or seven words per line and no more than six or seven lines per visual

Ex 8.2

- Do not over-use your visuals; your training should not be one visual after the other (approximately one every 1-3 minutes depending on the content and length of the presentation)

- Use color; color has a greater impact than black and white, but make sure you have distinctions between colors (approximately 20% of people have color-blindness and cannot distinguish all the colors of the continuum)

- Use visuals only when it is pertinent to the point you are making; people distract easily, so remove it once the point has been made

- When using numbers or bullets (best way to list key points) make sure there are at least two or more points, otherwise use paragraph form

- Use capitalization prudently

    o Capitalize the first letter of each word in titles, except for articles (the, a, an, etc.)

    o Capitalize only the first word of each bulleted point, except for proper nouns

        ▪ Do not capitalize generic names of departments, products, and positions

- Limit fonts to no more than two styles on a slide – usually one for the title / heading and one for the text

- Use emphasis-type appropriately

    - **Bold**: for headings and captions
    - *Italics*: for book titles and non-standard English words
    - Underlined: for hyperlinks – do not use, if possible
    - Color: for slides – use black for transparencies and printed text; avoid blue (used for hyperlinks)
    - ALL CAPS: for abbreviations and acronyms; capitalization is more difficult for participants to read – it also denotes "yelling"

- Use animation sparingly
- Make visuals available to participants; participants want and expect copies of the visuals – you must determine, however, whether to distribute them before or after the presentation. One option is to include them in the appendix of the participant workbook.

> If overused, animation can become annoying, or at best distracting. Swooshing and typing sounds and the animation of one word or one line at a time can create irritation rather than interest.

Flipcharts

Flipcharts are still quite effective for use with small groups of 25 or less, and for capturing feedback during group discussions.

Prepared flipchart pages are used the same as slides and transparencies, but present a more casual format. Not only do pre-written flipcharts serve as visuals for the participants, but as notes and reminders for the instructor.

When using blank pages for collecting feedback from the group, write exactly what is said without translating. If the response is too wordy, ask the participant to summarize his/her point. If the participant has difficulty with this, ask permission to summarize, and then verify that you have captured his/her thoughts correctly.

Tips for Using Flipcharts:

- Draw with letters 2 – 3 inches high for visibility
- Use up to six lines of content per page
- Use an empty sheet between each prepared sheet to avoid "bleed-through"
- Keep your torso facing the audience even when writing; do not face or talk to the flip chart when writing

- Alternate colors by line for easy reading; save reds for emphasis
- Pause long enough for participants to copy notes before flipping pages
- Avoid using the bottom of the page – participants seated further away will not be able to see this information

Review Quiz

1. Visuals must be visible, legible, and clear. Describe what is meant by visible;

   _____

   _____

2. What number of participants is most appropriate for using flip charts? _____

3. You do not want to over-use your visuals. How many slides should you use per 1-3 minutes? _____

Fill-in the blanks

4. Experts estimate that individuals retain only _____ of what they hear and _____ of what they see and hear.

5. Visuals enhance the content by stimulating the participants' _____ – using colors, pictures, sound, and animation.

6. _____ have become the preferred method of creating and projecting visuals, therefore slides (often on PowerPoint) are the most common format for visuals in corporate training.

7. Limit titles to _____ words or less.

8. There should be only _____ or _____ words per line and no more than six or seven lines per visual.

---

1. To have all letters and graphics seen from even the back of the room; 2. 25 or less; 3. One; 4. 10 – 20%; 30 – 50%; 5. Senses; 6. Computers; 7. Five; 8. Six, Seven

Personal Notes

Tool Nine: Evaluation

In her book *Measuring The Impact Of Training*[1], Pamela Wade states, "The ultimate measure of success of any training effort is whether the organization is better off after the training than it was before training began."

There are many ways of evaluating the success of your training efforts, including capturing the reactions of the participants immediately following the training, and comparing productivity and service reports post-training. One of your most effective comparisons, remember, is measuring how close you came to the "desired state" of your original needs assessment (tool#2), and how many of the identified barriers were addressed and eliminated after training was completed. In order for your evaluation to truly be valid, it must be tied to your needs assessment.

The success factors of your training must always be a part of the development process and planning: where you're going, and how you'll know you've successfully arrived. This means having a plan to evaluate your effectiveness during (case studies, exercises, skill practice, etc.), at the end of the training (questionnaires), and after the participants have returned to the job (observation, survey, performance statistics). What you measure depends on your organization's need, and the scope of the training.

Why evaluate?

Training should be evaluated on several levels and at different times during and after the session in order to answer the following questions:

- Is this the right approach for solving the issue(s)?

- Does the training achieve the objectives that were set forth?

- Does the training provide added value to the participants; the team; the organization?

- Where does the program itself need improvement?

- Is this the right format for the subject matter?

- How much of the information have the participants retained?

[1]*Richard Chang publishing, 1995*

The most widely used model for evaluating training was introduced in 1959 by Donald Kirkpatrick. It describes four levels of evaluation that have become the standard criteria for evaluation: *reaction, learning, behavior, results.*

Kirkpatrick's Levels of Evaluation

Level 1: Reaction

This first level evaluates the participant's reaction to the learning experience, and where the popular "smile sheet" is used. The term "smile sheet" was coined because the one-page questionnaire captures the feelings and thoughts of the audience in terms of whether they liked the program and liked the instructor.

Many trainers disregard the importance of the "smile sheet" because they assume it only gauges the "fun-factor" of the class. This may be true of a poorly constructed evaluation sheet, but the Level One evaluation can provide very important feedback with the right questions being asked.

Although Level One evaluations cannot measure the level of learning or the participant's ability to transfer knowledge back to the job, it will provide the trainer with ideas for improvement and the overall perceptions of the audience as to the effectiveness of the training. This is an opportunity to ask participants about the content, the materials, the methods and formats used during the session, the learning environment, and the instructor – all important to assess.

Kirkpatrick believed that you should not bypass Level One evaluation because, as he put it, "If they do not react favorably, they will not be motivated to learn.[2]"

Level 2: Learning

Level Two's purpose (*learning*) is to measure the level of success the instructor had in delivering the content, the degree to which the participants have retained that content, and whether the objectives of the course have been met.

This evaluation is assessed both during and after the training, using success indicators such as skill demonstrations, pre-post tests, role plays, and exercises – any method that confirms the participant's ability to perform.

Studies show that a significant number of organizations utilize Level One and Level Two evaluations. However, according to the American Society for Training and Development (ASTD) industry best-practices report of 2005 and 2006, the trend is shifting from program-level evaluation to metrics that measure business impact and organizational value.

[2](1994). *Evaluating Training Programs*

Level 3: Behavior

This level measures the degree learning has been transferred from the training environment to the job. The evaluation is conducted approximately three to six months after the program has been completed. Methods for measuring behavior change include:

- Observation
- Interviews
- Skill Assessments
- Performance Reviews
- Surveys

Level Three evaluation can be time consuming and costly, and requires an organized and well-planned follow-up strategy. The success of the training program, however, is predicated on the participant's ability to utilize the information / skills on the job – all would agree. Consequently, this level of evaluation would be well worth the effort. The value of uncovering barriers that impede application would be priceless data for the improvement and future success of the program.

Once the behavioral data has been collected and processed, communicate your results with managers and appropriate shareholders.

Level 4: Results

Level Four is the most difficult and expensive evaluation to conduct, and is therefore not appropriate for all training programs. Its objective is to measure the impact of the learning experience on the company's bottom-line - determining if the benefit of the training out-weighs the cost of its implementation, and to what extent it has contributed to the organization.

This evaluation is difficult because there are so many factors that influence the participants' results after the session has ended, and the complexity of isolating the learning from these factors. Nevertheless, to conduct this level of evaluation, you must review the data accumulated during your initial needs assessment; the areas of measurement must be the same as those originally identified. In other words, your success factors must have been determined from the beginning.

Measuring *results* may include the following methods:

- Sales increase
- Turnover rates
- Safety records
- Customer satisfaction
- Employee satisfaction
- Error rates
- Productivity rates
- Operating costs

As learning and development becomes more integrated with business strategy, the more training professionals use higher levels of evaluation and the more sophisticated the metrics. The 2006 ASTD report indicates that the best companies have (or are in the process of creating) dashboards and scorecards to monitor the effectiveness of training. This also helps to validate training as a fundamental driver of behavior change which, in turn, drives performance. As a result, training executives are able to manage the learning function as a business.

Review Quiz

1. According to Pamela Wade, what is the ultimate measure of success of any training effort?

   _____

2. What is the most widely used model for evaluating training?

   _____

3. What are the four levels of evaluation?

   1)

   2)

   3)

   4)

Matching

_____ 1. Level One

d) This level measures the degree learning has been transferred from the training environment to the job. The evaluation is conducted approximately three to six months after the program has been completed.

_____ 2. Level Two

e) This level evaluates the participant's reaction to the learning experience. It will provide the trainer with ideas for improvement and the overall perceptions of the audience as to the effectiveness of the training.

_____ 3. Level Three

f) This level's objective is to measure the impact of the learning experience on the company's bottom-line - determining if the benefit of the training outweighs the cost of its implementation, and to what extent it has contributed to the organization.

_____ 4. Level Four

g) The purpose of this evaluation is to measure the level of success the instructor had in delivering the content, the degree to which the participants have retained that content, and whether the objectives of the course have been met.

1. Whether the organization is better off after the training than it was before training began; 2. Kirkpatrick's model; 3. Reaction; learning; behavior; results; Matching 1.b; 2.d; 3.a; 4. c

Personal Notes

Tools in Action Review

There is an order – a logic - to creating and executing a successful training program. By following the Cycle of Training Effectiveness (exhibit 10.1), you will eliminate frustration and "re-dos" when establishing your development program and ensure the best return on your time and resource investment. This cycle is the start-to-finish process of successfully implementing a program.

Ex. 10.1
The Cycle of Training Effectiveness

1. NEEDS ASSESSMENT
2. ANALYZE RESULTS
3. CREATE PLAN
4. FOCUSED PREPARATION
5. EXECUTE PLAN
6. MONITOR & COACH
7. EVALUATE RESULTS
8. COMMUNICATE & CELEBRATE

Review Exercise

Instructions: Each of the 8 steps in the Cycle of Training Effectiveness will necessitate the use of one or more of the *Tools of the Trade*. Review the details of each step and identify the tools that you would use from the previous chapters, to be successful. (You may discover more tools than indicated in the answers – the more the better.)

1. ***Conduct a Needs Assessment:*** Identify the problem; clarify "desired state;" collect "current-state" data from organization, incumbent groups, and stakeholders; conduct a gap analysis (compare current state to desired state); establish strong business partnerships;

    - Tool: _____
    - Tool: _____

2. ***Analyze the results of your assessment:*** Sort data; conduct qualitative and quantitative analysis; brainstorm /propose solutions with business partners; communicate results to shareholders; determine next steps.

    - Tool: _____
    - Tool: _____

3. ***Create your plan:*** Determine desired outcomes; prioritize the "Whats" (the content for the training); identify the specific "Whos" (the appropriate participants / audience); determine "Hows" (sequence and method(s) of delivery); identify success criteria, and evaluation tools.

    - Tool: _____
    - Tool: _____
    - Tool: _____

4. ***Focus your preparation:*** Create content, facilitation guides, and participant materials; partner with senior management and end-users; identify subject-matter-experts (as needed); train trainers; identify results indicators for individual courses; determine training formats and methods; secure resources/equipment; arrange administrative support.

    - Tool: _____
    - Tool: _____
    - Tool: _____

5. ***Execute the plan:*** Train; manage; provide necessary support; follow up with stake holders; respond to immediate feedback with adjustments to the program as needed.

   - Tool: _____
   - Tool: _____
   - Tool: _____

6. ***Monitor the progress of the learning and coach facilitators when necessary:*** Stay engaged.

   - Tool: _____
   - Tool: _____

7. ***Evaluate your results:*** Compare results against success criteria.

   - Tool: _____
   - Tool: _____

8. ***Communicate and celebrate:*** Report results to "shareholders" and Recognize Contributors

   - Tool: _____
   - Tool: _____

1. A needs assessment instrument or internal process; An occupational analysis; **2.** Scope and Sequence; Personal Presence for presentations and reports; **3.** Learning Objectives; The Training Plan; Program Objectives **4.** Instructional Methods; Master Mixes; Visual Aids **5.** Personal Presence; Instructional Methods; Evaluation Level 1 **6.** Level 1 Evaluation; Personal Presence **7.** Level 2-4 evaluation; Learning Objectives **8.** Presentation and reports; Personal Presence

Personal Notes

Case Study: The Diversity Training Project

In response to customer and employee feedback that strongly implied a discrepancy in service and treatment, I was asked by senior management of a national organization to create a diversity awareness training program that would educate and increase sensitivity towards ethnic and cultural diversity. I had just completed two weeks of diversity education and communication training at the Summer Institute of Intercultural Communication (SIIC) in Oregon, and the organization felt this was a great opportunity to get a return on their investment.

After the request, I met with my boss and the two champions of this project (Sr. VP of Human Resources and the Chairman) to clarify the outcomes and expectations of the diversity training they'd asked for. In other words, I needed to fully understand what they wanted to be different in the thinking, perceptions, and behaviors of employees once the training was completed.

After some discussion, the objectives we agreed upon were as follows:

- All employees would see, hear, and understand the company policies and values concerning diversity.

- Employees would have a common definition of diversity throughout the organization.

- Customer and employee complaints concerning diversity issues would be reduced (and eventually become non-existent).

- Employees would feel valued and appreciated.

The expectation was that training would be rolled-out to all employees: all regions; all levels; all departments, and delivered in a format that would be easy to understand and assimilate. This would be a first. There had not been any training program in the company's history that had been rolled-out to the entire organization – lucky me.

Building a Team

When I accepted the training assignment, I was a project team of one. I was also smart enough to know that *that* was a formula for failure of disastrous proportions. Even with champions in "high places," I needed partners and buy-in from the bottom-up and across all business units.

Having been associated with the company for a number of years, combined with reading many of the customer comment cards and letters, I had a fairly good idea of what some of the issues were, but I also needed verification of my assumptions. My first "ask for help" went out to the Diversity Committee, which was a grass-roots committee of both hourly and salaried employees.

I explained the project, and asked that they partner with me as advisors and information gatherers. The group was excited to participate, and used their departments, business units, and internal networks to validate the issues, confirm or nullify assumptions, and uncover additional concerns. In addition to their informal assessments, we conducted focus groups and gathered customer impact data from the marketing department.

During the process of this initial needs assessment, the committee was reorganized and I was invited to become a member. Overnight I had a team.

The Assessment

Once the assessment data was in, it revealed several concerns:

- When discussing diversity, many were still using the term "affirmative action."
- Minority employees felt disempowered and were de-motivated because of a lack of people-of-color in senior positions.
- Diversity, for many meant black and white.
- Customers and employees of color believed they were stereotyped and profiled by security, and therefore treated differently.
- There was a general sense of distrust in senior management to do anything differently, and to respond with positive action when discrimination issues were raised. Many believed nothing would change.
- Quite a number of people were uncomfortable when immigrant employees communicated with each other in a language other than English.
- Women believed there was still a "glass-ceiling," while people of color believed there was a "brick ceiling" ...and so on.

I met with my stakeholders to present the assessment results, refine the objectives where needed, and discuss my recommendations for going forward. (This was provided both verbally and in writing.) The plan was to create a 90-minute inter-active awareness program that would present the "business case" for valuing diversity, and communicate the company position and values concerning each employee and customer. The program would also include an internally-produced video that could be used as a "stand-alone" for future new-hire orientations.

We discussed using the video format to re-emphasize the corporate values and policies and to make the impact of diversity "real" by re-enacting several customer service "boo-boos" identified in the assessment as examples of inappropriate behavior. We decided to utilize internal talent (without the aide of any professional actors / actresses), and represent as many "faces" of diversity as possible: race, gender, age, life style, ethnicity, organizational and company position, and geographical culture, in the production.

Deal. We all agreed, and the work began.

Please understand that a 90 minute diversity program was NOT going to change an organization's culture, neither was it expected to make major changes in behavior. It was designed to be a beginning coversation – a first step in awareness. At the same time, the RIGHT message spoken at the RIGHT time in the RIGHT environment can change an individual's belief and/or perspective which can lead to a change in behavior. If this were not so, why would ministers spend hours preparing to deliver a 45-60 minute sermon week after week?

As trainers, it is an all-to-familiar scenario that we are asked to present 4 hours worth of content in 30 minutes (somewhat exaggerated but not much) to an audience of 100 when the optimum classroom size is 25-30. Sometimes with the right "evidence" from our analysis, we can increase the time we have allotted and reduce class size, but there are also circumstances in which we cannot. It is then that we must be smart enough to make the content and its delivery as powerful as possible, and to "set-up" the learning in advance of the experience. This case study was a classic example, and here's what I mean:

In understanding that this training was to be delivered throughout the organization, I knew just by doing the math (dollars per hour per person away from their job /office, plus overtime for some, plus hours per day per facilitator, plus travel), that 2 hours would be the maximum amount of time I'd have for the actual training experience. Therefore, in order to begin the "message," of diversity inclusion, I used the assessment-stage as an opportunity for people to share their feelings and perspectives, and to begin the dialogue for understanding the impact of diversity in the present culture. This happened in the focus groups.

Each focus group included individuals of different backgrounds, organizational levels, ethnicities, genders, ages, and any other dimensions of diversity we could put together. The conversations all began with an introduction as to what we were wanting to accomplish and why (which included the company's values and philosophy), then the trained facilitator took notes, asked questions, and let the communication flow from person to person. In other words, the focus groups were the first step in the training/awareness process.

This created a "buzz" in the organization as those who were a part of the groups began to discuss their experience with others. The next opportunity to educate came with the filming of the video.

There were approximately 35 – 40 employees included in the video. The importance of valuing diversity and diversity inclusion was repeated over and over, and the participants not only spoke the words, but walked through the scenarios many times. (When working with non-professionals, the re-takes are countless. Do you think that was by accident?)

During and after the video experience (it was a first-time for many) the participants could not stop talking about it both at work and at home. (Several of those who were involved in this process told me what a difference it made in their understanding and in their heart.) This was the next step in the learning process – not by happenstance, but by purposeful intent!

Author's Note: *In my opinion, a trainer / facilitator must NEVER approach a learning opportunity by thinking that 1 hour or 2 hours, or 8 hours won't matter. If you believe this, you'll be right: it won't matter and you won't make a difference.*

You have the tools, and you have the power to MAKE it matter. If you only have an hour, make sure that you don't over-promise the outcomes of course, but by-golly <u>*make that the most insightful hour ever-known-to-man.*</u> *Make sure that your content is straight-forward and meaningful (no fluff), your delivery is exemplary, and that they can see and experience the message in you. (Remember tool #1? It's YOU.) If, on the other hand, you believe it's impossible to deliver outcomes given the time allotment, just say "no."*

For this diversity training I thought it through, mapped it out, uncovered the less-obvious learning opportunitites, and believed I could make a difference. Although I only had 90 minutes of "air-time," I discovered that I had 60 hours or more of contact / impact time available.

Can you make a difference in 60 hours? Absolutely you can. It's a change of mind-set: how can you maximize your "full" opportunity, not just classroom, or webinar, or video time!

Show and Tell

I sought assistance from a local diversity consulting group – Tom Nesby and Associates – and with Tom's help and the training I'd received from PhDs Lee Gardenswartz and Anita Rowe at SIIC, I was able to develop the training content, video script, collateral materials, visual aides, and program roll-out strategy.

Once the program was written, exercises created, and the video edited and completed, I asked if I could use the executive committee as the training pilot group. I wasn't sure if it was because it was a great idea, or because I used senior management in the video, or because they were shocked that I asked - that they agreed.

The pilot was very successful, and several members of the executive committee voiced praise for the program. Then the comment came that I was hoping for:

"Linda, if there's anything we can do to ensure the success of this training, "please let us know." The statement was primarily rhetorical, I believe, but I took them at their word.

"Thank you so much," I said, as I looked each one in the eye and smiled.

"And yes, as a matter of fact, there *is* something you can do: you can show your commitment by volunteering to co-facilitate this program."

I let a brief moment of silence hang in the air and nodded ever so slightly at my stakeholders, before continuing.

"It would take months to deliver multiple sessions of this training to all 40 of our remote locations plus the entire corporate office, by myself. I also have great concerns about delivering this as an African American female without a partner – someone either male, or Caucasian. It's important that we eliminate all speculation that I may have ulterior motives for doing this, or that I am delivering on a personal soapbox.

"If we truly believe in the message of appreciating diversity, we need to demonstrate it in the delivery as well. Let's show diversity successfully working together and agreeing together on this subject, starting at the very top.

"We have already identified several potential facilitators from HR and the diversity committee, and I am asking that each of you volunteer to co-facilitate with either myself or one of the other facilitators. I will provide several train-the-trainer opportunities for you to practice and become comfortable with the content, and oh by the way, I promise to make you heroes, and not let you fail.

"So, what-do-you-say?"

With that last statement they chuckled. The Sr. VP of Marketing (one of my personal champions), shouted "What a splendid idea!" and I received nearly 100% participation. That day, the size and "clout" of my team experienced a major growth spurt.

Relationship Building

With the successful roll-out of the diversity awareness program, my training partners and I developed strong business relationships of trust and respect throughout the organization.

True to my promise, the members of the executive team *did* become heroes of a sort. The employees were duly impressed with a leadership team that believed valuing diversity was important enough to personally meet with them to talk about appreciating the diversity that each of them brought to the table. Each group and location also received a copy of the video as a training tool to use for new-hire orientation, and the training lived on for a number of years.

Follow Up

Needless to say, the training program could not address every issue and concern that was identified during the assessment. Some of the issues could not be solved with training solutions, while others were more appropriate for follow-up sessions or for integration into management / supervisory skills training.

To further increase our understanding of the organization's diversity issues, we asked participants to give feedback on the program and identify other areas of diversity we should address. We received lots of feedback, and gained a greater understanding of the diversity concerns throughout the organization. This sparked the fuel for future learning and communication opportunities, and laid the ground work for many to later become involved in other company training programs.

I believe the success of the corporate-wide diversity training program moved the company out of its traditional training comfort zones into a new way of thinking and behaving.

Training and development had previously been the sole responsibility of human resources, but the diversity program changed the mind-set from training being the role of a departmentally few, to becoming everyone's responsibility.

For Discussion

1. Do you think an assessment was needed when senior management already knew what training they wanted, and had given a clear directive? Why? Why not?

2. A training assessment's purpose is to identify the training needs that will help solve business problems (it uncovers what may be causing the problem). What was / were the business problem(s) the diversity program was designed to solve?

3. From the assessment data, which issues could possibly be solved by training, and which ones could not? How would you handle the non-training issues?

4. The statement was made that being a team of one was a formula for failure. Why do you think that would be true? Why not?

   What would have been different without a team?

5. Do you believe asking members of senior management to co-facilitate the training created a risk? Why? Why not?

   What were the up-sides and down-sides to having them involved that closely?

6. What would you have done differently if the assignment had been given to you?

7. What were your most valuable learning points from this example?

"Greatness is not in where we stand, but in what direction we are moving. We must sail sometimes with the wind and sometimes against it – but sail we must and not drift, or lie at anchor."

Oliver Wendell Holmes

Tools of the Trade

Case Study: The Making of a Training Academy

I learned during my early years of retail that corporate training could come and go depending on who owned the company and whether sales were up or down. There also seemed to be a 5-7 year life expectancy for the training department (not really good for job security) so depending upon when you were hired during the "cycle," your training experience could vary significantly. Consequently, when I was hired in 1979 as a part-time holiday sales associate, and then received five days of training at the corporate office downtown, I knew business must have been going pretty well.

The corporate trainer's persona made quite the impression: she was a beautiful, well dressed Asian-American woman; knowledgeable, graceful, proficient. She also taught all the courses in the curriculum, which I found unusual. (Was there only one trainer?) Although I felt she was an average facilitator (not too boring, not too engaging – a little impersonal perhaps), she represented the company very well professionally. (I never expected training to be interesting:, I just expected it to be thorough.[1]) As a minority female, however, she *did* give me hope that I too, had the potential of making great wages as a corporate trainer (and to be able to dress like her), with opportunities for advancement. I was "jazzed." I knew then that I wanted to be in training: I'd found my calling. Little did I know, however, that the training department would disappear within months, and another decade would pass before I would join the training team.

Once the formal training was completed, I returned to my local store and received informal training in the form of mentoring. I was so impressed that I stayed on as a full-time sales associate for another seven years (it was a long holiday season).

Historical Perspectives

Soon, sales associate training was reduced to one day in the local stores and taught by the Personnel Department. (This was before the term "human resources.") Department Sales Managers still received technical and supervisory skills training however- but regionally rather than centrally. Corporate managers, on the other hand, were sent to external seminars on an individual bases if they *really* needed it, or lobbied for it.

---

[1] *As a baby-boomer, the expectations for training were practical. My generation did not expect to be romanced or entertained, but to be sufficiently equipped to perform our jobs effectively. Times have changed. The generations called GenY and Millenniums expect a sufficient amount of training, and for it to include high-tech multi-medium integration, be fun and engaging, and prepare them for both their present and future job needs. This has had a huge impact on current training formats and methodologies.*

In order to help keep my dream alive, I volunteered to be a new-hire trainer in my store and was granted permission to do so- even though I wasn't in personnel (consequently, my hopes for being a well dressed corporate trainer who made a lot of money, began to diminish considerably).

By the time I resigned to teach junior high school in 1986, training had been reduced to a notebook and few hours of classroom. Throughout the organization training was provided on very limited basis, usually implemented from an "oops-let's-fix-that" approach, rather than "just-in-time."

Technology Re-awakens Training

In 1989 I returned to the world of retail after a turbulent divorce, working evenings while I continued to teach during the day. I found that corporate training had re-emerged with the dawning of new technology. As the company began its slow transition from manual to electronic applications, there arose an increased need for training. Computer systems were put in place for the buyers, the marketing department, and for bridal registry, and because of this, a technical trainer was hired to deliver all systems and computer applications training in the corporate office.

In Search of Best Practices

As was the the experience of many retailers, there seemed to be a consistent pattern of mergers and acquisitions. Our company was no exception. Before long, it too was purchased by a larger conglomerate.

In order for this new organization to maximize the training that already existed throughout its recently acquired divisions, and to standardize core competencies across business units, training executives from the national office set out on a road-tour to identify training best practices. They visited each of the regional corporate offices and interviewed senior VPs of HR and their training teams.

Our division didn't exactly have a training team, but *did* have the technical trainer and a few other individuals who were responsible for a number of training functions, including customer service training, training manual development, product knowledge, and sales procedures.

The National Training Team

When the best practice assessments were completed, the national office asked each division to participate in the continued standardization by placing their highest-level training person on a newly formed all-divison team of training professionals. In consideration of the request and anticipation of increased training responsibilities for the division, our senior management selected a corporate training manager.

In addition to being the primary facilitator for all "soft-skills" (non-technical) training, the training manager also became our division's representitive on the national team. As a member, this person would help analyze the data from assessments and provide feedback and recommendations from focus groups and various subject-matter-experts.

Although disappointed not to have been selected, I already had other responsibilities as the Executive Placement Manager for the stores. Because of this, I watched our involvement with the national training team from afar.

The Call

"Afar" became an understatement, for I was being romanced by another company, and left to be the western regional training manager for a light manufactoring and wholesale company. It was a blissful marriage of sorts until I got the "call," the following summer.

"Linda, this is Greg. So are you ready to come home?" asked my previous boss.

"Home? *Oh No!* Is something wrong with my kids? What happened? Oh wait... how did you get my number here in Denver? I'm in a hotel for heaven's sake! Greg Anderson? Is this you?!?"

Needless to say, I was surprised to hear his voice on the other end of the line.

Greg chuckled and said, "I *always* know where you are, and how to get a hold of you. So like I said, are you ready to stop fooling around and come back?"

"Are you kidding me?" I laughed. "*Surely* you jest!"

"No, I'm serious," he said. "You've had your chance to spread your wings a little, now it's time for you to come back where you belong."

"Greg," I replied "I already belong. I belong here," and laughed. "I really appreciate this, you know, but there's no way I can return. You don't have a position for me."

"Yes I do, or I wouldn't be calling."

"You may *think* so, but I know that you don't."

"I'm not following you," he said.

"There's only one position I'd be interested in, and there's already somebody in it."

"That may have been the case," Greg explained, "but the position is now open."

I went on to explain that although the training manager position may have been open (I knew which one he was referring to), the level of the position was too low. I wasn't interested in being a training manager. I already *was* one. I had a huge amount of reponsibility and atonomy, and the salary was great – no complaints.

"Sorry," I said "but I appreciate the call anyway. You made me feel very special, thanks."

"We're not through talking yet," Greg responded. "When do you get back to Seattle?"

I told him, and we agreed to talk again. I'd always liked Greg, and I'd enjoyed having conversation with him, but I had <u>no</u> intention of returning.

I was flattered by Greg's phone call, but also wondered what was *really* going on. I decided to tap into my network of friends to get the "real scoop" when I returned.

Negotiations

When we finally talked, Greg drove a hard bargain and made it difficult for me to say "no." He knew that the "hook" would take more than wages and benefits (although those were very important), and he painted the picture for me that was hard to resist: The training department had been created not long after I left, but unfortunately, (to put it tactfully) it imploded on itself because of poor-decision making by a few individuals on the team. The smoke was still clearing even as we negotiated my return.

One full-time manager and a part-time adminstrative assistant were all that remained of the department, and in the absence of direction and over-sight, the stores had begun "doing their own thing."

"Oh, so you want me to come back to fix it?" I asked more of a statement than a question.

"Exactly."

We both laughed, and I said I'd think about it. I told him that I wasn't sure I wanted to do clean-up work and walk into a undesireable situation, but the truth was, he'd baited me with a strong hook.

As the reader, you may think that the situation surrounding this case study is getting somewhat personal. The truth is, the situation was and is <u>extremely</u> personal. There were extenuating circumstances behind my leaving in the first place – not just because of another company "romancing" me away - and I knew that returning would carry a lot of emotional baggage – if I let it.

The question was: "Could I put it aside and do what I do best for the sake of the company I had worked for so long?"

The answer to that was "No."

The next question was: "Could I harness my emotional energy into strong motivation that would allow me to accept this new situation as the ultimate challenge and demonstrate what I had in talent, skills, and knowledge to exceed expectatons and create as many heros and s/heros along the way – as a sense of <u>personal</u> gratification?"

To that, the answer was "Ab-so-lute-ly!"

Am I saying that the "work" of a training professional needs to be personal and something more than tools and techniques? No, not necessarily, but if you want to move beyond the ordinary to something extraordinary, there must be an element of passion.

Consider the philosophy of Jim Collins , author of <u>Good to Great:</u> Value-based companies (those that balance monetary ideals with emotional / people ideals) are the longest lasting companies. They demonstrate that employees are driven by idealism and emotion, and in turn, create <u>greatness</u> by putting meaning and purpose into their work (passion).

The understanding is that human beings simply will not perform well for any length of time without meaning and purpose – this is definatley me, and in this scenario, I had gained purpose in abundance.

I had developed a <u>passion</u> for training and development, and a care and concern for those with whom I'd worked. Could one create a phoenix from ashes? I believed so. I also believed people could excel and move from "good to great" with increased skill and motivation, and I was willing to answer that call.

Make it So

In late fall, I returned as the Director of Training, and was greeted by balloons, flowers, cards, and big hugs from several well-wishers throughout the day. It felt wonderful, but I also wondererd if this was an indication that everyone (but me) knew how difficult my job was going to be!

Greg and I agreed that I would have a separate training budget, hire an additional training manager to oversee department manager and "Stores" training (not just a specialist), be able to purchase the necessary equipment and tools that were lacking, and have enough atonomy to do what was necessary for restoration without being entangled in political "red-tape." He would continue to be training's and my champion. My only directive from "above" was to make it happen: put the training department "back on the map," and have it be one the company could proudly rely on. (Easy for them to say.)

Building the Team

My first task was to rebuild the training team and create for them a sense of safety and trust. Individually, I took my two remaining direct-reports to lunch in order for us to get acquainted, and to hear from their perspective what happened to the department and how they felt about it. I asked for their help and partnership in rebuilding the department, and for their willingness to allow me to lead them through the process.

My one manager, Michelle, literally said, "Yeah boss sure," with a warm smile, and added "but it won't be easy." My administrative person explained to me that her commitment was only to stay on board until a new boss was hired. She'd already found another job and was leaving. There was nothing I could say or do. She appreciated the lunch, but wanted me to consider that her official two-week's notice.

Because my return and new position had been announced electronically throughout the organization, I had two immediate items on my "to-do" list: fill the open positions on my team, and communicate to the stores, buyers, planners, and corporate managers what they could expect from the newly organized training department. (I wanted to post a big sign outside our area which said "Under New Management," but I thought that might be tacky.)

I've always believed it was important to lead by example, so I made sure that I had a diverse pool of candidates before making a hiring decision. I used formal channels through human resources for internal and external candidates, but also used informal recruiting: word of mouth and networking.

Because of the many partnerships and network channels, I had a wide selection of talented applicants. With buy-in from Michelle, (my only other team member remaining) Joanne was hired to manage the "Stores" training, and Diane accepted the administrator's position. Both women were external hires, and I announced them to the company with a promise that we would listen to their needs and provide quality training to meet those appropriate needs. Thus began our internal marketing campaign.

Assessments

The first thing I needed to know was what was currently happening in training. I understood that the stores were "doing their own thing," but I needed to know what those "things" were and why they were happening. My training managers and I held focus groups – Joanne in the stores, Michelle in the buying offices, and me in the corporate areas – to ascertain the current state of training, to identify other needs that were left unmet, and to find out what was working and what wasn't. In addition to the focus groups, we read exit interviews, employee surveys, and evaluation feedback ("smile sheets") from previous training classes.

We discovered that stores training in the regions were inconsistent in both content and delivery, and according to Christine, VP of Human Resources, training happened sporadically, and led to "no where" in particular.

"There was no path that training created or led to," explained Christine. "People believed it was necessary when it happened, but you'd find opinions to be different depending on who you talked to."

I met with Greg and asked for time on the executive committee's meeting agenda to discuss their views of the organization's training needs. During that meeting we also talked about training's impact on the business, and although the group believed there was at least some minimal antidotal impact, there was no data to support it.

Thanks to the training teams at the national level, competencies for department sales managers and assistant buyers had been established, and a skills assessment had been created to measure the level of proficiency for those two major groups.

The skills assessment was a great tool. The problem was that it wasn't being utilized consistently, and where it *was* being used, the results went "no where." It was meant to be a developmental tool, of course, so the results only mattered to the few who cared about developing their people – or who "had time." Nevertheless, we collected all the assessment data available to help us with our gap analysis.

In the meantime, calls were coming in for us to travel to the regions for management training; the buyers were calling for training for their new assistants; corporate directors and department heads were calling requesting team building and supervisory skills training for their people, and there were only four of us – three trainers and an administrative assistant (which also explained why many departments were "doing their own thing").

A New Direction

My team and I were working so hard and fast trying to keep up with requests that we were not able to be proactive. Neither were we able to assess our effectiveness, nor utilize the information from all the data we'd pulled together. We felt that we were just the servant responders to the requests, ideas, and whims of others. To say the least, we all had high expectations for ourselves, so although we'd only been together as a team for less than six months, we felt frustrated and unsuccessful.

The four of us met in my office for one of our weekly meetings and agreed that the run-a-way train had to stop. Following this decision we began the "what ifs:"

- What if we "blew up" the existing training norms and started over?

- What if we developed training partners – subject matter experts – to help us deliver training in all areas?

- What if, instead of creating conflict with those "doing their own thing" for their *own* people, we organized all the existing programs and institutionalized them under one umbrella?

- What if employees got "credit" for training as part of their performance appraisals?

- What if the subject-matter-experts got credit and recognition for being trainers?

- What if the company considered being a subject-matter-expert trainer a developmental opportunity?

- What if training classes directly related to business profitability and the individual's promotability?

- What if training was so integrated in the organization's business success, and its systems, that to eliminate the training department would be to unravel part of the company's business strategy and culture?

- What if we could create a training department that lasted years after we were gone?

- What if we could get the entire company excited about training?

- What if we made a decision to "just do it?"

The more we talked, the more excited we became. We looked at each other and laughed with nervous anticipation.

"So?" I said

"Listen you guys, we can *do* this!" Joanne said half shouting.

Diane giggled and nodded her head saying "Ok, sounds like fun. Ok everybody?"

Michelle was smiling all the while and responded "Sure. *I'm* in. Let's do it!"

I was also smiling with pride and the pure exhilaration of having a team that was willing to take risks and to pioneer. The buy-in added fuel to the vision.

"All right," I said. "For the next couple of weeks let's suspend the running around and concentrate on changing the paradigm. If you can't change your schedule for a promised training class, do what you need to do, but our objective is to recapture training and institutionalize it; to make it significant and make it 'stick'.

"We're going to create a training department that won't burn down!" I exclaimed. And with that we "high-fived" all around.

The Plan

"So what do you suggest as our first step?" asked Joanne.

"Good question," I said. "Who has a model we like and want to emulate?"

We decided on the community college model. Diane had been an administrative assistant at a junior college prior to joining us, so we asked if she would make some calls to registrars, program directors, and anyone else who would be willing to let us buy them lunch in exchange for a little administrative education. Our greatest resource came from the Continuing Education Department at one of our local community colleges, and its director, Richard, who helped us understand the college's business and curriculum structure, enrollment process, and marketing strategies.

In less than a month we had a plan. We'd researched and identified all the training that was taking place outside of our department, who was teaching what, who the high-potential subject-matter-expert trainers were, and what core competencies we could effectively address given the present resources. We'd also drafted a sample Schedule of Classes (using the community college model) to show how all the pieces would fit together. Oh yes, we were *very* excited over the possibilities.

The next step was to "pitch" our idea to Greg, then to the executive committee. The team had done their due-diligence and completed a cost and benefits analysis for making this change, and worked out the preliminary logistics for registration and enrollment. We were ready.

Buy-in and Partnership

True to his commitment, Greg was Training's champion, and was a huge supporter and champion of the recommended new format. Our idea was to create a corporate university with all the success factors and evaluation metrics built-in. Even with the enthusiasm over the suggested restructuring, his position was very clear: we were in the retail business and were a resource and supporter of that business by providing the necessary training and development for growth and profitability, not in the training business which happened to support the activities of retail. That was clearly understood.

With team members present, I made the presentation to the executive committee. It was fairly short, but to the point. It included:

- The overview results of our needs assessments;

- The short-term and long-term objectives for creating our own corporate university solution, including potential barriers;

- The results of the cost and benefits analysis;

- The proposed metrics and success factors;

- What we needed from them to ensure win-win success.

After handing them a detailed report, including our recommended plan for logistics and developing more trainers to meet the increased need (without adding payroll, by the way), we engaged in a lively discussion.

Although I'd done my fair share of "pre-selling" the idea to individual members of the committee prior to the meeting, I was surprised with the overall level of receptivity. There was an enthusiastic and unanimous decision to "make it so," even when it included increasing my budget to accommodate the new plan.

Let me just interject a word about "pre-selling:" I learned a long time ago from one of my mentors - a respected senior executive - never to present anything that is a *surprise* to senior management. The key was to inform them individually (if at all possible) of what you intend to present, bullet-point the benefits to them and their business units (address the WIIFM), ask for their input and feedback as to how to make your idea more business-applicable, and ask if there is any reason they would hesitate to give their support. If there is, let them know that you will address the issue, and thank them for their partnership. In other words, you "sell" your idea in advance and person-to-person before the big meeting.

The whole conversation should take no more than 15 minutes, and you've improved your presentation and increased your influence and support in one swoop.

During my presentation, the one additional request the committee made of me was to create tests that employees would have to pass as a requirement for successfully completing their curriculum courses.

The one additional request I made of *them* was to respond with positive affirmation if they were invited to sit on the board of our new school. (We had not organized the board yet, but we *would*, and we didn't have a name for our little corporate university, but that was next on the list.)

Oh yes, I almost forgot: I also asked them for a building to house our school, but they said "No" without hesitation. (I felt that I needed to give them something to reject.) With the exception of the building, we all agreed, and my team and I "made it so" in thirty (30) days.

Preparation

There was a lot for us to do, so we divided the work-load:

- We identified the criteria and skill competencies for subject-matter-expert trainers, and set team expectations for ourselves; (see Appendix pgs 114-115)
- Subject-matter-experts (SMEs) were recruited and trained
    - Many stepped forward, having been involved in our initial focus groups
    - We provided orientation, adult learning principles, and presentation skills training
    - All trainers, including those in our department, received training in writing effective tests questions and formats
    - We renamed the SMEs "faculty"
    - Our team of trainers grew from a team of three to seventy-two
- We announced our new format and launched a contest to create a name for our new "school;"
    - A manager in the accounting department submitted a most appropriate name and won!
- The Academy Board of Directors was formed as an accountability group, and to provide advice and secure resources when needed;

- A Schedule of Classes was created and distributed as a marketing tool and registration information document;
    - The Schedule included classes being offered by other departments outside of our training department and integrated them into academy offerings
- A data base was created to track participant course completion;
- Training and conference rooms were painted, prepared, and reserved for the "opening," and hotel accommodations were secured for out-of-town participants.

The Opening

Although the first classes held through the Academy were those already available through the buyer, planning, stores, and systems training programs, it began with appropriate fanfare. Senior management addressed the participants and shared lunch with them, catering prepared special treats, and several individuals were interviewed by the communications manager for an article to be published in the company's news magazine.

While the summer opening was successfully commencing, the fall schedule was being created. Train-the-trainer classes were being held for new SMEs, and preparations for the new quarter were being organized, including a limited number of night classes. It was a new day and a legacy was in the making.

The Report

A full issue of the news magazine was used to introduce the Academy prior to the fall quarter of classes. This turned the summer quarter into a "soft opening," and fall into the official opening and announcement. The internal publicity accelerated the sense of significance and permanency of training in its new format.

It communicated our objectives as a training organization, but also publicized the benefits to the participants who would attend. In addition, it served to unify the training efforts of all departments. In an instant, the Academy became the "umbrella" for all training in the corporation.

Growth

Less than a year after the Academy opening, the training department began to experience rapid growth in curriculum offerings, team members, and SMEs.

Rebecca came aboard as the Corporate Training Manager and continued to develop and expand the corporate manager's training curriculum, creating also the first formalized corporate orientation program. In addition, the product knowledge, sales specialist, planner, and systems training managers joined as "official" training team members.

As I mentioned, the team of subject-matter-experts continued to grow, and to recognize their contribution and continue their development, we created a training Camp. Camp was a "themed" day of fun and development, focused on the SME. Members of senior management would often participate in recognizing the valuable contributions of the trainers and the presenting of awards and prizes - which were plentiful. In Michelle's words: "Incentives and praise really worked to retain the faculty and make the employees feel special. It took just a little honey to sweeten the pot."

It was important to us that our trainers, whether SME "extended faculty" or full time facilitators, taught classes with a consistency of skill and professionalism. It was just as important to us that they also benefited from the wide internal network available to them, and Camp was the ticket.

It's important to understand also, that the training team participated in numerous development opportunities throughout our years together. In fact, it was difficult to retain team members because other executives wanted to promote them out of the department to work for them. In one sense the department was a "farm" - growing future senior executives.

Certification and Articulation

The relationship with the community college remained strong. After two years, I believed we were ready to take our training academy to the next level, so I contacted the community college again. I met with Richard, and asked what it would take for our employees to get college credit for completing our Academy courses and curriculum. This was another one of my 'What ifs" that I had secretly dreamt. I wanted our people, who had not completed their college education, to be able to get a "jump start" and the motivation to complete their degree by attending our academy. It could easily be a two-for-one situation: attending the training Academy was mandatory for managers, and since the classes were on company time, why not also earn college credit towards that degree? Surely this was far beyond the expectations of the functions of corporate training, but "why not?"

For articulation (being joined or interrelating to college curriculum for credit), our courses had to pass certain content criteria and evaluation standards, and had to relate to, or be compatible with courses offered in a degree program at the college. Ok, we could make that happen...

Then I was asked about the training credentials of our trainers. Well, that was another matter. As far as I knew, none of the training staff (or SMEs) had a degree in education or was (at a minimum) certified as a vocational education teacher. This was potentially a problem.

After a brief discussion with Greg and the team, we decided to take the leap from "pretty- great-all-ready" to "standard-setting greatness," and have the training team members state certified as vocational education teachers.

This was a two-year venture of commitment, with every member of the team studying together under the tutelage and instruction of our college teacher, Laura[2] who we grew to love and respect.

At this time, there were eight full-time members of our team; everyone, including our administrative assistant, graduated from the program with honors, and was certified. Greg, together with the company president, our CEO, and Richard from the college, recognized and congratulated the team with a small reception, to which spouses and family members were invited.

Simultaneously, work was being done to articulate our courses, and by graduation day, several of our classes had completed the scrutiny of standards and content, and had been articulated. With this announcement, employees could enroll for on-line classes through the Academy and receive college credit for many of our leadership and management courses, facilitated by training team members.

Conclusion

From ashes to phoenix - it *is* possible. A small team of individuals captured the vision, released the passion, and reclaimed the integrity and respect of their department. Training changed from being a reactionary group of classroom facilitators, to a developmental institution with learning professionals and organizational business partners.

My mission there was complete.

---

[2] *Laura was diagnosed with cancer in the spring of our final year of certification. Although it had aggressively progressed to final stages, she refused to transfer the responsibility of our education and training to anyone else. She even conducted our last class session while bedridden. Laura passed away days before we received our certificates.*

For Discussion

1. In your opinion, to what degree did the "heat" of emotion and passion play in leading the transformation of the training department into a Training Academy?

2. The new training team waited almost six (6) months before re-engineering the department. Do you believe that was too long? Too short? Or unnecessary?

   What would you have done and why?

3. There were many different assessment methods used to determine the existing state of training within the organization. In your opinion, why were so many necessary, or why not?

   Were there any secondary benefits to conducting the needs assessment?

4. From your perspective, what was the significance of the training team's "what if" conversation?

5. Discuss what you believe the leadership strategy was toward the training team, and why it was, or was not effective?

6. What factors do you believe contributed to the training team being able to execute the roll-out of a training academy in thirty (30) days?

7. What, if any, were the risks in articulating parts of the training curriculum for credit, and certifying the training team as vocational ed. teachers?

   What position would you have taken?

8. What are your views on "pre-selling" your ideas to senior management before making a presentation? What would you have done differently to ensure buy-in? Why?

Personal Notes

Appendix

Tips for Conducting Focus Groups

- ☐ Send out focus group questions, assessment instruments, or skills inventories to your participants in advance, so they have time to think about their answers.

- ☐ Assure the group that they will remain anonymous – specific comments will not be associated with any one person. Let them know that their ideas will help in the development of training.

- ☐ Record job titles and length of time on the job, on a sign-in sheet.

- ☐ Set an informal atmosphere to encourage discussion. (Snacks?)

- ☐ Have plenty of flipchart paper available to record information. Consider having two people conduct the focus group – one to facilitate discussion and one to record information.

- ☐ Move from general to specific and probe for answers.

- ☐ If discussion becomes negative, redirect the group by asking, "What could be done to improve this situation?"

- ☐ Be careful not to reject or negate anything someone offers.

- ☐ Do not become defensive or ask leading questions.

- ☐ Recorder should periodically check to be sure he/she is recording the participant discussion accurately.

- ☐ Don't let the group get off target; redirect the group to its focus.

- ☐ Give the group an opportunity at the end to add any comments or ideas they haven't stated.

Training Curriculum Inventory
(Of Existing Programs)

Training Program	Hours	Outcomes	Trainer	Target Audience	(Cost per Person)	Delivery Format

Training Plan Worksheet
(Sample "A")

NEED (TYPE OF TRAINING / DEVELOPMENT)	AVAIL Y / N?	AUDIENCE	AUDIENCE	AUDIENCE	AUDIENCE	AUDIENCE	AUDIENCE

TRAINING PLAN WORKSHEET (Sample "B")

Job / Position: _____

Program Objective / Outcomes: _____

_____

Prerequisites: _____

COMPETENCY/ SKILL	LEARNING OBJECTIVE	COGNITIVE OUTCOMES	LEVEL / SEQUENCE	FORMAT(s)	ASSESSMENT/ RESULTS INDICATOR

Training Practices Check List*

This check list can be used to identify the strengths and weaknesses of your training practices. Just as evaluating participants is vital to the learning process, evaluating yourself allows you to achieve and maintain top performance.

	Yes	No
Did you make the objective(s) clear?	☐	☐
Did you make the session participatory?	☐	☐
Did you provide your learners with an agenda and stick to it?	☐	☐
Did you encourage questions?	☐	☐
Did you avoid antagonizing, condemning, losing patience with, or embarrassing participants?	☐	☐
Did you have an effective opening and closing?	☐	☐
Did you gear the session toward learners' needs?	☐	☐
Did you promote networking among participants?	☐	☐
Did you use visuals and a variety of learning methods?	☐	☐
Did you check the facility in advance?	☐	☐
Did you dress professionally?	☐	☐
Did you evaluate learners' performance?	☐	☐
Did you start on time?	☐	☐
Did you move around the room?	☐	☐
Did you keep discussions on track?	☐	☐
Did you stay interested in the material?	☐	☐
Did you vary your method of delivery?	☐	☐
Did you structure your "persona" appropriately for the situation?	☐	☐
Did you remain calm?	☐	☐
Did you maintain an appropriate level of eye contact?	☐	☐
Were your gestures in sync with your words and message?	☐	☐

* Modeled from ASDT *"Dos and Don'ts for the New Trainer"*

Participant Evaluation Sheet

Program / Course: _____

Instructor: _____ **Date:** _____

Please rate your learning experience by checking the appropriate box below.

Perception	5 Excellent	4 Very Good	3 Good	2 Fair	1 Unacceptable
1. Overall quality of program					
2. Application to work environment					
3. Value of program concepts and materials					
4. Trainer's ability to present content and respond to the needs of the group					

Written Comments:

What did you discover that you can immediately apply?

What would you have liked to have spent more / less time on?

Other comments:

SKILL COMPETENCY ASSESSMENT FOR STAFF TRAINERS

JOB PERFORMANCE

Y	N	MINIMUM REQUIREMENTS
		Score of 3.5 or higher on annual performance appraisal
		In Good Standing within Organization
		Has positive relationships and credible reputation with key "stakeholders" in the Organization
		Has strong team relationships and skills
		Is a "change advocate"

GENERAL ABILITIES / CHARACTERISTICS

Y	N	CHARACTERISTICS / COMPETENCY
		Has a passion to help people advance in both knowledge and skills
		Has strong inter-personal / people skills
		Is a strong and effective communicator
		Is self-confident and self-reliant
		Is able to address difficult issues and resolve conflict speedily
		Is able to inspire others into action
		Is considered by others to be a good leader
		Is able to work well under stress and think / respond quickly on his/her "feet"

KNOWLEDGE

Y	N	COMPETENCY
		Has minimum 1 year working-experience / knowledge in area in which training will be conducted
		Has "Mastery-level" understanding in primary area in which training will be conducted

FACILITATION SKILLS

Y	N	COMPETENCY
		Has the ability/ skill to effectively utilize training "tools:" PowerPoint, Flip Charts, Leader's Guides, etc.
		Is able to "manage" a large group of participants, including leading games, exercises, and handling negative behavior and group challenges
		Is able to "engage" participants in learning
		Is able to "lead" others into a higher "comfort-zone" level throughout the learning process
		Is able to influence, and gain buy-in from participants

PRESENTATION SKILLS

Y	N	COMPETENCY
		Is able to make the subject-matter interesting
		Is able to motive people to action
		Is able to link learning to practical day-to-day business applications
		Is able to "read" an audience and make immediate changes to content, process, and techniques when necessary

"Real inspiration must come from within. If there is nothing within, nothing from outside can help, The best poetry, the greatest of painting, the sublimest of nature cannot produce any worthwhile result if the divine spark of creative faculty is lacking within the artist."

Sergei Rachmaninov

References and Resources

REFERENCES

Carliner, Saul (2003). <u>Training Design Basics</u>. ASTD Alexandria, VA 22313

Dowling, Ellen. (1993). <u>The Standup Trainer</u>. ASTD Alexandria, VA 22313

Gardenswartz, Lee and Rowe, Anita (1993). <u>Managing Diversity</u>. New York: Irwin

Hart, Lois (1991). <u>Training Methods That Work</u>, California: Crisp Publications

Kirkpatrick, Donald. (1994). <u>Evaluating Training Programs</u>, San Francisco: Berrett-Koehler

Lawson, Karen (1998). <u>The Trainer's Handbook</u>. San Francisco: Jossey-Bass Pfeiffer

Leatherman, Dick ((1990). <u>The Training Trilogy: Assessing Needs</u>. Massachusetts: HRD Press, Inc

Prince, Don W (2000). <u>Communicating Across Cultures</u>. North Carolina: Center for Creative Leadership

Sparhawk, Sally (1995). <u>Identifying Targeted Training Needs</u>. California: Richard Chang Associates

Wade, Pamela (1995). <u>Measuring the Impact of Training</u>, California: Richard Chang Associates.

Zemke, Ron and Kramlinger, T. (1982). <u>Figuring Things Out</u>. Massachusetts: Addison-Wesley.